2

A Communicative Course in English

Sandra Costinett
with Donald R. H. Byrd

Donald R. H. Byrd *Project Director*

Anna Veltfort *Art Director*

Longman

Library of Congress Cataloging-in-Publication Data

Costinett, Sandra.
    Spectrum 2, a communicative course in English / Sandra Costinett
  with Donald R. H. Byrd; Donald R. H. Byrd, project director; Anna
  Veltfort, art director.
      p   cm.
  Also published in a two-book split edition
  ISBN 0-13-829979-X
    1. English language--Textbooks for foreign speakers.   I. Byrd,
  Donald R. H. II. Title. III. Title: Spectrum two.
  PE1128.W359 1993
  428.2'4--dc20
                                                              92-47370
                                                                 CIP

    ISBN (2A) 0-13-829987-0   ISBN (2B) 0-13-830027-5

Project Manager: Nancy L. Leonhardt
Editorial Project Directors: Karen Davy and Larry Anger
Assistants to the Editors: Andrew Gitzy, Stephanie Karras, Sylvia P. Bloch

Production Manager: Sylvia Moore
Production Editor and Compositor: Jan Sivertsen, Ken Liao
Technical Support and Assistance: Molly Pike Riccardi and David Riccardi
Production Coordinator: Ray Keating

Cover Design: Roberto de Vicq
Interior Concept and Page-by-Page Design: Anna Veltfort
Audio Program Producer: Paul Ruben

ACKNOWLEDGMENTS

Illustrations: Storyline illustrations by Anna Veltfort: pages 1–4, 8–9, 18–19, 28–29, 40–41, 54–55, 64–65, 74–75, 90–91, 100–101, 110–111, 120–121, 134–125, 144–145, and 154–155; pages 14, 16 (bottom), 27 (top), 31–33, 35 (top right), 37, 60–61, 77–80, 84, 93–95, 140–141, 150, and 157–160 by Anne Burgess; pages 88 and 114–115 by Laura Freeman; pages 88, 123–125, 148–149 by Hugh Harrison; pages 21–23, 66, 117 and 138–139 by Randy Jones; pages 5, 15, 36, 57–59, 85, 96, 109, 127–129, 142, 143, and 151 by Gene Meyers; pages 34 and 35 (top left) by Ivor Parry; pages 6, 16 (top), 24, 25, 27 (bottom), 43, 45–46, 50 (bottom), 51 (top), 63 (top), 70 (bottom), and 73 by Chris Reed; page 89 by Philip Scheuer; pages 26, 38–39, 50 (top), 62, 63 (bottom), 71, 99, 116, 130, 152, and 153 by Arnie Ten; and pages 106 and 133 by Leyda Torres.

Photos: Page 6 (top and middle right) by Marc Anderson; pages 6 (bottom right) and 92 by Laimute E. Druskis; page 6 (bottom left) by Mike Kagan/Monkmeyer Press; pages 6 (middle left) and 30 UPI/Bettmann; page 6 (top left) The Pennsylvania State University Still Photo Department; pages 10, 11–14, and 17 (left) by Rhoda Sidney; pages 16, 17 (middle and right), 47–49, 67–69, 81–83, 103–105, 124, 141, 150, and 156 by Susan Oristaglio; page 20 Reuters/Bettmann; page 52 (Honolulu) Hawaii Visitors Bureau; page 52 (Canada bottom left) by Thomas Kitchin/First Light; page 52 (San Francisco top) by Susan McCarteny/Photo Researchers; page 52 (San Francisco middle) by Lawrence Migdale/Photo Researchers; page 52 (San Francisco bottom) by Will and Deni McIntyre/Photo Researchers; page 52 (Montreal top) by Joseph Nettis/Photo Researchers; page 52 (Canada top right) by Porterfield/ Chickering/ Photo Researchers; page 52 (Canada bottom right) by G. Zimbel/Monkmeyer; page 52 (Montreal middle and bottom/Canada top left) courtesy of Quebec Tourism; page 76 by Tom Zimberoff/SYGMA; pages 77–78 by David Sailors/The Stock Market; page 86 (left) Index Stock Photography; page 86 (right) and page 122 (Wright Brother's plane, astronaut, and Bell telephone)Archive Photos; page 102 by Jon Eisberg/FPG International; page 112, and 136 Globe Photos; page 118 (top, middle, and bottom left) Uniphoto; page 118 (top right) by Mark Reinstein/Uniphoto; page 118 (middle right) by R. Lee/ Uniphoto; page 118 (bottom right) by Art Stein/Photo Researchers; page 122 (Edison lamp and early televisions) Culver Pictures; page 122 (Halogen lamp) by Brownie Harris/The Stock Market; page 118 (video telephone) by Bill Nation/Sygma; page 118 (hand–held TV) by Michael Keller/FPG International; page 131 Sportschrome; page 133 by Richard Rodaman; page 146 (left) courtesy of the United States National Museum; page 146 (middle) courtesy of Lexus; page 146 (right) courtesy of General Motors; and page 148 by Richard Laird/FPG International.

Realia: Page 7 (bottom) by Jan Sivertsen; pages 7 (top), 16, 20, 30, 42, 44, 51, 52, 53, 56, 62, 66, 72, 77, 78, 85, 86, 87, 92, 99, 102, 106, 118, 119, 122, 123, 124, 125, 126, 131, 132, 136, 156, 159, and 160 by Siren Design.

© 1994 by Prentice Hall Regents
A Pearson Education Company
Pearson Education, 10 Bank Street, White Plains, NY. 10606

ISBN 0-13-829979-X

INTRODUCTION

Welcome to the new edition of *Spectrum! Spectrum 2* represents the second level of a six-level course designed for adolescent and adult learners of English. The student book, workbook, and audio cassette program for each level provide practice in all four communication skills, with a special focus on listening and speaking. Levels 1 and 2 are appropriate for beginning students and "false" beginners. Levels 3 and 4 are intended for intermediate classes, and 5 and 6 for advanced learners of English. The first four levels are also offered in split editions—1A, 1B, 2A, 2B, 3A, 3B, 4A, and 4B.

Spectrum is a "communicative" course, based on the idea that communication is not merely an end-product of language study, but rather the very process through which a new language is acquired. *Spectrum* involves students in this process by providing them with useful, natural English along with opportunities to discuss topics of personal interest and to communicate their own thoughts, feelings, and ideas.

In *Spectrum*, understanding a new language is considered the starting point for communication. The student books thus emphasize the importance of comprehension, both as a useful skill and as a natural means of acquiring a language. Students begin each unit by listening to and reading conversations that provide rich input for language learning. Accompanying activities enhance comprehension and give students time to absorb new vocabulary and structures. Throughout the unit, students encounter readings and dialogues containing structures and expressions not formally introduced until later units or levels. The goal is to provide students with a continuous stream of input that challenges their current knowledge of English, thereby allowing them to progress naturally to a higher level of competence.

Spectrum emphasizes interaction as another vital step in language acquisition. Interaction begins with simple communication tasks that motivate students to use the same structure a number of times as they exchange real information about themselves and other topics. This focused practice builds confidence and fluency and prepares students for more open-ended activities involving role playing, discussion, and problem solving. These activities give students control of the interaction and enable them to develop strategies for expressing themselves and negotiating meaning in an English-speaking environment.

The *Spectrum* syllabus is organized around functions and structures practiced in thematic lessons. Both functions and structures are carefully graded according to simplicity and usefulness. Structures are presented in clear paradigms with informative usage notes.

This student book consists of fourteen units, each divided into one- and two-page lessons. The first lesson in each unit presents a series of authentic conversations, providing input for comprehension and language acquisition. A preview activity prepares students to understand the cultural material in the conversations. New functions and structures are then practiced through interactive tasks in several thematic lessons. A two-page comprehension lesson provides further input in the form of a dialogue, pronunciation activity, listening exercise, and a role-playing activity—all related to the storyline for the level. The final lesson of the unit presents authentic documents such as advertisements and news articles for reading comprehension practice. There are review lessons after units 4, 7, 11, and 14. An accompanying workbook, audio cassette program, and teacher's edition are available.

For the preparation of the new edition, Regents/Prentice Hall would like to thank the following long-time users of *Spectrum*, whose insights and suggestions have helped to shape the content and format of the new edition: Motofumi Aramaki, *Sony Language Laboratory*, Tokyo, Japan; *Associacão Cultural Brasil-Estados Unidos (ACBEU)*, Salvador-Bahia, Brazil; *AUA Language Center*, Bangkok, Thailand, Thomas J. Kral and faculty; Pedro I. Cohen, Professor Emeritus of English, Linguistics, and Education, *Universidad de Panamá*; *ELSI Taiwan Language Schools*, Taipei, Taiwan, Kenneth Hou and faculty; James Hale, *Sundai ELS*, Tokyo, Japan; *Impact*, Santiago, Chile; *Instituto Brasil-Estados Unidos (IBEU)*, Rio de Janeiro, Brazil; *Instituto Brasil-Estados Unidos No Ceará (IBEU-CE)*, Fortaleza, Brazil; *Instituto Chileno Norteamericano de Cultura*, Santiago, Chile; *Instituto Cultural Argentino Norteamericano (ICANA)*, Buenos Aires, Argentina; Christopher M. Knott, *Chris English Masters Schools*, Kyoto, Japan; *The Language Training and Testing Center*, Taipei, Taiwan, Anthony Y. T. Wu and faculty; *Lutheran Language Institute*, Tokyo, Japan; *Network Cultura, Ensino e Livraria Ltda*, São Paulo, Brazil; *Seven Language and Culture*, São Paulo, Brazil.

UNIT	PAGES	THEMES	FUNCTIONS
1 Lessons 1 – 6	1–10	Greetings Introductions Personal information Housework Sports and leisure-time activities	Greet someone formally Introduce someone formally Greet someone informally Find out where someone lives Talk about housework Talk about sports Talk about leisure-time activities Talk about frequency
2 Lessons 7 – 11	11–20	Appointments Health Advice Job skills Abilities	Introduce yourself to a receptionist and give the time of your appointment Talk about health problems Offer sympathy Give and accept advice Talk about abilities
3 Lessons 12 – 17	21–30	Offers Problems Suggestions Telephone calls	Ask what someone is doing Offer help Talk about a problem Make a suggestion Make a telephone call Get a wrong number Remind someone
4 Lessons 18 – 24	31–42	Shopping Clothing Locations Colors Opinions Compliments Past activities Furniture	Shop for clothes Talk about location Talk about color and size Talk about fit Ask for an opinion Return something to a store Compliment someone Talk about the past Ask about store hours Identify items Talk about price
Review of units 1 – 4	43–46	Review	Review
5 Lessons 25 – 29	47–56	Instructions Office machines Future plans The seasons and weather Invitations Excuses	Give instructions Talk about future plans Talk about the seasons and the weather Invite someone informally Give an excuse

S E Q U E N C E

LANGUAGE	FORMS	SKILLS
I'm Charles Jackson, the new teller. Oh, yes. How do you do? Charles Jackson, I'd like you to meet Larry Silver, our loan officer. Larry Silver, Charles Jackson, our new teller. Hi. Are you Charles? Yes. What's your name? I'm Patricia, but everybody calls me Pat. Nice to meet you, Pat. Where do you live, Charley? In Highland Park. How about you? Just a few blocks from here./On Grand Street./At 338 Grand Street. Do you like to cook? I like to cook, but I don't like to do the dishes. Do you play any sports? I like to swim. How often does Sue read? Hardly ever. Oh, about once a week.	Nicknames Prepositions *in, on, at* with addresses Verbs followed by infinitives Frequency adverbs and expressions	Listen for a name and a time Listen to the intonation of short statements Read a newspaper article Write a letter to a friend (workbook)
My name's Van Horn. I have an eleven o'clock appointment. How do you feel today? My feet hurt. I've got a headache. I've still got a sore throat. That's too bad. What should I do for a stomachache? Maybe you should see a doctor. You should take aspirin for a headache. That's probably a good idea. Can you use a computer? I can type, but I can't use a computer. Daniel has good office skills, so the doctor should hire him. The doctor should hire Daniel because he has good office skills.	Parts of the body Review: *have got* *Still* *Should* Review: impersonal pronoun *you* *Can* *So* and *because*	Listen to someone complaining about health problems Listen to a job interview Listen to a loudspeaker announcement Read a magazine article Fill out a job application form (workbook)
What are you looking for? A telephone. There's one right there. Who are you looking for? A waitress. I don't see one. I'll go and look for one. I'll go look for one. I'll come and help you. I'll come help you. What's wrong? The phone isn't working. The elevator doesn't work. Why don't you try again later? Let's go find another one. Good idea. Hello. Could I speak to Cory, please? Who's calling? Lee Watson. Hold on, please. Could I speak to Cory, please? There's no one here by that name. Sorry. I'm waiting for you at the theater. Did you forget our date?	Review: the present continuous Verbs and prepositions *Go* and *come* with and without *and* Equivalent uses of the present continuous and simple present	Listen to suggestions Listen to vowel and consonant reduction and blending in *got to, got a, get a* Read a biographical article Write about a famous person (workbook)
I'm looking for a sweatshirt. They're over there, by the tank tops. They're in front of the shoes. They're in back of the jackets. Any particular color? Yes. Navy blue. What size do you wear? A medium. How do the shorts fit? They're not tight enough. They're too big. What do you think of this tank top? It seems a little tight. I'd like to return this tank top. Would you like to see a different style? No, I don't think so. Thanks. Yes, please. Those sunglasses look good on you. Were they expensive? No, they weren't. They were on sale. How late are you open, please? Until 9:00. I like that chair. Which one? The striped one. The one across from the sofa. How much does it cost? $349.99. It's on sale.	Prepositions of location: *in front of, in back of, by* Colors and clothing sizes *Too* and *enough* Sense verbs + adjectives The past of *be*: yes-no questions *Which* Indefinite pronouns *one* and *ones*	Listen for locations Listen to a description of clothing Listen to a contrast of the two *th* sounds Read a short historical text Write about your favorite room (workbook)
Review	Review	Review
Put the document you want to send here. Don't put newspaper into the machine. When are you going to go to Montreal? In the winter. Are you going to go out? Yeah. I'm going to go shopping. What's the weather like in the winter? It's cold and snowy, so I'm going to go skiing. What's it like out? It's snowing. Do you want to come along? Sure. I'd like to, but I have to wait for a phone call.	The affirmative and negative imperative Preposition *into* The future with *going to* The seasons and the weather	Listen to instructions Listen for names of cities Listen to formal/informal pronunciations of *going to* Read a magazine article Write about plans (workbook)

P R E V I E W

FUNCTIONS/THEMES	LANGUAGE	FORMS
Greet someone formally	I'm Charles Jackson, the new teller. Oh, yes. How do you do?	
Introduce someone formally	Charles Jackson, I'd like you to meet Larry Silver, our loan officer. Larry Silver, Charles Jackson, our new teller.	
Greet someone informally	Hi. Are you Charles? Yes. What's your name? I'm Patricia, but everybody calls me Pat. Nice to meet you, Pat.	Nicknames
Find out where someone lives	Where do you live, Charley? In Highland Park. How about you? Just a few blocks from here.	Prepositions *in*, *on*, *at* with addresses
Talk about housework	Do you like to cook? I like to cook, but I don't like to do the dishes.	Verbs followed by infinitives
Talk about sports	Do you play any sports? I like to swim.	
Talk about leisure-time activities Talk about frequency	How often does Sue read? Hardly ever.	Frequency adverbs and expressions

Preview the conversations.

Everybody calls Charles Jackson by his nickname, Charley. Do people use nicknames or full names in your country? Do you have a nickname?

Charley plays soccer every week and Teresa plays tennis once or twice a week. What about you? Do you play any sports?

1. Just call me Charley.

Charles Jackson works as a bank teller in Los Angeles. His bank has just transferred him to another branch.

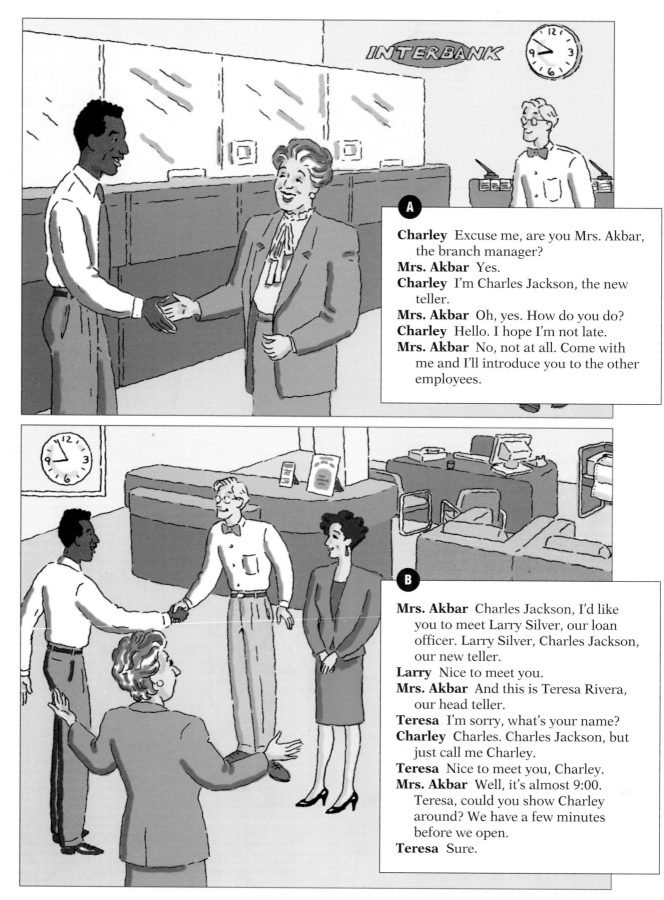

A

Charley Excuse me, are you Mrs. Akbar, the branch manager?
Mrs. Akbar Yes.
Charley I'm Charles Jackson, the new teller.
Mrs. Akbar Oh, yes. How do you do?
Charley Hello. I hope I'm not late.
Mrs. Akbar No, not at all. Come with me and I'll introduce you to the other employees.

B

Mrs. Akbar Charles Jackson, I'd like you to meet Larry Silver, our loan officer. Larry Silver, Charles Jackson, our new teller.
Larry Nice to meet you.
Mrs. Akbar And this is Teresa Rivera, our head teller.
Teresa I'm sorry, what's your name?
Charley Charles. Charles Jackson, but just call me Charley.
Teresa Nice to meet you, Charley.
Mrs. Akbar Well, it's almost 9:00. Teresa, could you show Charley around? We have a few minutes before we open.
Teresa Sure.

C

Charley That was a long day. I'm tired.
Teresa Yeah, and I have to go home and make dinner.
Charley Do you cook every night?
Teresa Yeah. I usually make dinner, and my roommate washes the dishes. Do you like to cook?
Charley Not really, so I eat out a lot. Fortunately, there are some good restaurants in my neighborhood.
Teresa Where do you live, Charley?
Charley In Highland Park. How about you?
Teresa Oh, just a few blocks from here.

D

Teresa Are you going to the gym now?
Charley No, I've got a soccer game tonight.
Teresa Oh, really? Do you play on a team?
Charley Yeah. We play every week. We're not very good, but we have a lot of fun. How about you? Do you play any sports?
Teresa I usually play tennis once or twice a week.
Charley What about you, Larry?
Larry No, I'm not too interested in sports. Sometimes I watch baseball on TV, but that's about all.

Figure it out

1. Listen to the conversations and match the people with their jobs at the bank.

1. Mrs. Akbar
2. Teresa Rivera
3. Larry Silver
4. Charley Jackson

a. teller
b. loan officer
c. head teller
d. branch manager

2. Listen again. Then say *True, False,* or *It doesn't say*.

1. Mrs. Akbar knows Charley very well. *False.*
2. Larry and Teresa are good friends.
3. The bank opens at 9:00.
4. Teresa is married.
5. Charley doesn't like to cook.
6. Larry loves to play sports.

2. Excuse me, are you Mrs. Akbar?

GREET SOMEONE FORMALLY • INTRODUCE SOMEONE FORMALLY

   1   ▶ **Listen to the two possible conversations.**
▶ **Imagine this is the first day of your new job at Interbank. Use your own name and greet the other employees.**

A Excuse me, are you Mrs. Akbar, the branch manager?
B No, I'm not. Mrs. Akbar is over there.
A Thank you.

A Excuse me, are you Mrs. Akbar, the branch manager?
B Yes.
A I'm Charles Jackson, the new teller.
B Oh, yes. How do you do?
A Hello.

Mr. Lawrence Silver
Loan Officer

Mr. John Wong
Assistant Manager

Mrs. Elizabeth Akbar
Branch Manager

Mr. Charles Jackson
New Teller

Miss Teresa Rivera
Head Teller

INTERBANK

   2   ▶ **Listen to the formal introduction.**
▶ **Imagine you work at Interbank. Use your own names and introduce two of the other employees to each other.**

A Charles Jackson, I'd like you to meet Larry Silver, our loan officer. Larry Silver, Charles Jackson, our new teller.
B Nice to meet you.
C Nice to meet you, too.

GREET SOMEONE INFORMALLY • FIND OUT WHERE SOMEONE LIVES

   3   ▶ **Listen to the conversation.**
▶ **Act out the conversation using different names from the list.**

A Hi. Are you Charles?
B Yes. What's your name?
A I'm Patricia, but everybody calls me Pat.
B Nice to meet you, Pat. Just call me Charley.
A Where do you live, Charley?
B In Highland Park. How about you?
A Oh, just a few blocks from here.

Some names and nicknames	
Richard	Dick (Rick)
Robert	Bob
Christopher	Chris
Christine	Chris
Elizabeth	Liz
Susan	Susie (Sue)
Lawrence	Larry
Teresa	Terry

4   ▶ **Greet a classmate and introduce yourself. Find out where your classmate lives.**

Prepositions with addresses
In Highland Park.
On Grand Street.
At 338 Grand Street.

3. Do you like to cook?

TALK ABOUT HOUSEWORK • VERBS FOLLOWED BY INFINITIVES

🔊 **1** ▶ Everyone in this family helps with the housework. Listen to what each person says and match the statements with the correct pictures.
▶ Make a list of other things you have to do around the house.

1. I make (cook) dinner. _e_
2. I wash (do) the dishes. ___
3. I set the table. ___
4. I make the bed. ___
5. I clean the house. ___
6. I do the laundry. ___

a

b

c

d

e

f

🔊 **2** ▶ Listen to the conversation.
▶ Act out the conversation with a partner, asking about the housework in exercise 1.

A Do you like to cook?
B Not really. How about you?
A I like to cook, but I don't like to do the dishes.

3 ▶ Study the frame.

Verbs followed by infinitives			
Do you **like to cook**? Yes, I **love to**. (Yes, I do.)	I	plan hate prefer want need have ('ve got) decided	to cook.

🔊 **4** ▶ Listen to the conversation and complete it.
▶ Practice the conversation with a partner.

A Do you _____ housework?
B Well, I _____ , but I _____ the laundry and things like that.
A I _____ and do laundry either.
B Do you _____ ?
A No, I hate to. I _____ in restaurants. In fact, I _____ out to eat tonight. Would you _____ me?
B I'd like to, but I _____ shopping after work. And then I _____ my sister at the movies.

5 ▶ Talk with a classmate. Find out two things your classmate likes to do around the house. Find out two things he or she hates to do.

4. What do you do in your free time?

1 ▶ Match the clues with the sports.
▶ Listen to check your answers.

1. Chris Thomas loves this sport, but it's dangerous. He has to protect his face and wear heavy clothes and gloves. He plays _b_ .
2. Liz Jenkins needs a ball and a club to play this sport, and she often plays alone. She plays ___ .
3. Maria Ortiz plays on a team. She uses a ball, and she runs and jumps a lot. She plays ___ .
4. Pat Dobbs uses a ball and runs a lot, but the ball for this sport isn't round. He plays ___ .
5. Lee Howard uses a round ball for this sport, but he can't use his hands. He plays ___ .
6. Sue Chen needs a small round ball and a racket to play this sport. She can't play alone. She plays ___ .

a. football

b. hockey

c. golf

d. soccer

e. tennis

f. basketball

2 ▶ Listen to the conversation.
▶ In groups of three, have similar conversations, using your own names and information.

A Do you play any sports, Teresa?
B I like to play tennis.
A How about you, Larry?
C No, I'm not too interested in sports, but sometimes I watch baseball on TV.

I like to swim.

I like to jog (run).

I like to ski.

I like to go to the gym.

I prefer to read in my free time.

3 ► Mark wants to know more about his friends. Listen to the conversation and check the appropriate box.

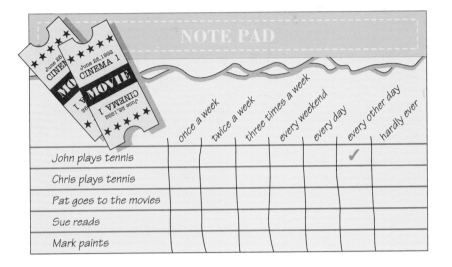

	once a week	twice a week	three times a week	every weekend	every day	every other day	hardly ever
John plays tennis						✓	
Chris plays tennis							
Pat goes to the movies							
Sue reads							
Mark paints							

4 ► Tell your classmates about your favorite sport or leisure-time activity.

A I play tennis once or twice a week.
B I like to read.
C I hardly ever do anything. I just don't have time.

5 ► Study the frame.

Frequency adverbs and expressions

How often does he play tennis?	He plays	every day. every other day. once a week. twice a month. three times a year. very often.	He	almost always almost never hardly ever seldom	plays after work.

almost always = usually
almost never = hardly ever = seldom

TALK ABOUT FREQUENCY

6 ► Elaine and Barry Dupont don't have a lot of free time. Work with a partner and look at the Duponts' calendar. Ask questions about their schedule.

A How often do Elaine and Barry have dinner with friends?
B Oh, about twice a month.
A How often does Elaine work late?
B . . .

FEBRUARY

S	M	T	W	T	F	S
1 Dinner with Barry's parents	**2** Go grocery shopping	**3** Barry: French class	**4**	**5** Go grocery shopping	**6** Elaine: late meeting at office	**7**
8 Play tennis 1–3 p.m.	**9** Go grocery shopping	**10** Barry: French class	**11** Elaine: late meeting	**12** Go grocery shopping	**13** Meet Mike and Sue for dinner	**14** Concert at Newman Hall 7:30
15 Dinner with Elaine's parents	**16** Go grocery shopping	**17** Barry: French class	**18**	**19** Go grocery shopping	**20**	**21**
22 Play tennis 2–4 p.m.	**23** Go grocery shopping	**24** Barry: French class	**25** Elaine: late meeting at office 5–7 p.m.	**26** Go grocery shopping	**27**	**28** Meet Chuck and Amy for dinner

Unit 1 **7**

5. I know what you mean.

Charley Jackson is picking up his friend Steve Kovacs, who owns an auto repair shop. Charley and Steve have a soccer game tonight.

1

Charley	Come on, Steve. It's time to go.
Steve	Wait a minute. I just have to close up the shop.
Charley	O.K.
Steve	By the way, can we give my sister a ride home tonight?
Charley	Sure. You mean she's coming to the game?
Steve	Yeah. She wants to take some pictures.
Charley	I didn't know Eva was interested in photography.
Steve	Yeah. She'd like to work for a newspaper someday.
Charley	Hmmm.
Steve	But I think she'll have a lot of competition. There are a lot of photographers out there.
Charley	Well, there's competition in everything we do.
Steve	I know what you mean. Did I ever tell you I wanted to be a professional soccer player?
Charley	You're kidding! *(Phone rings)*
Steve	Yeah. I did. Just a minute . . . Hello, Steve's Auto Repair . . .

2. Figure it out

True or *False*?

1. Steve owns an auto repair shop. *True.*
2. Charley and Steve both play soccer.
3. Charley has a sister named Eva.
4. Eva wants to be a photographer.
5. Steve wanted to be a professional soccer player.

3. Listen in

A man calls Steve about his car. Read the statements below. Then listen to the conversation and choose *a* or *b*.

1. The man's name is
   a. Young.　　　b. Yung.

2. Steve's repair shop is open from
   a. eight to six.　　b. six to eight.

4. Your turn

Bob Carter is a new mechanic at Steve's repair shop. He introduces himself to Margaret Morelli, the bookkeeper at Steve's. Act out the conversation.

Bob　Are you Margaret Morelli?
Maggie　————————————
Bob　Hi. I'm Bob Carter, the new mechanic.
Maggie　————————————
Bob　Nice to meet you, too, Margaret.
Maggie　————————————
Bob　O.K. . . . Maggie. So where do you live?
Maggie　————————————
Bob　I live on Clifford Street, too—near the park. In fact, I always play baseball there.
Maggie　————————————
Bob　Oh, once or twice a week. Do you play any sports?
Maggie　————————————

5. How to say it

Practice the conversation.

Steve　Charley, this is Bob Carter.

Charley　Hi, Bob.

Steve　And this is Margaret Morelli.

Charley　Hi, Margaret. Nice to meet you.

6.

Survey: How do you relax in your free time?

Here are a few examples of how people responded to this week's survey question. According to the answers, people's leisure-time activities are as varied as their jobs—some are typical, some unusual.

Jeffrey Knight, Advertising Manager, Today *Magazine*

I work in a very busy department—hectic, actually. I started scuba diving this year, and I love it. It's really beautiful under water. Why do I like it? Well, I'm always very rushed and tense at work. But when I dive, everything is so peaceful. Everything moves slowly and it's completely quiet. I go diving about twice a month. On the other weekends, I usually stay home and work in my garden.

Mary Jo Parker, Mother of Ryan and Derek Parker

Free time? Who has free time? I have two little boys—Ryan is four and Derek is two. And my husband often works overtime. When he works nights and weekends, I have to do all the housework and take care of the kids by myself. Sometimes I watch a video in the evening after the boys go to sleep, but usually I just fall asleep when they do.

Edith Shelton, Former English Teacher

I'm retired now, so I have a lot of spare time. I like to go to the community center and play bingo about four times a week. My grandchildren think it's funny that I play bingo so often. They call me "Lucky." Well, sometimes I win and sometimes I lose, but I always have a good time.

Yuki Yanisagawa, Mover

I work for a moving company and carry heavy furniture all week, so I hardly ever do anything on the weekend—except paint. It's very relaxing. I prefer to paint portraits. Sometimes I walk to the park on Saturday or Sunday and paint the people I see there. I'd like to be a professional artist, but I can't make a living that way.

1. **Read the article and find two other ways to say "free time."**

2. **Answer the questions.**

1. Which person doesn't have much free time?
2. What do the other three people do in their leisure time?
3. What does each person do for a living?

PREVIEW

FUNCTIONS/THEMES	LANGUAGE	FORMS
Introduce yourself to a receptionist and give the time of your appointment	My name's Van Horn. I have an eleven o'clock appointment.	
Talk about health problems	My feet hurt. I've got a headache. My throat still hurts.	Parts of the body Review: *have got* *Still*
Offer sympathy	That's too bad.	
Give and accept advice	Maybe you should see a doctor. You should take aspirin for a headache. That's probably a good idea.	*Should* Review: impersonal pronoun *you*
Talk about abilities	I can type, but I can't use a computer. Daniel has good office skills, so the doctor should hire him. The doctor should hire Daniel because he has good office skills.	*Can* *So* and *because*

Preview the conversations.

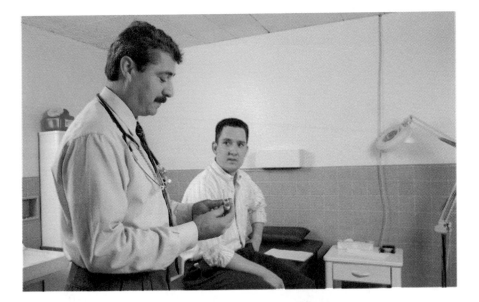

This patient went to the doctor because he has a headache and his throat hurts. When do you go to the doctor? Do you need an appointment?

7. How do you feel today?

Dick Van Horn doesn't feel well. He has an appointment with Dr. Valentine.

A

Receptionist May I help you?
Mr. Van Horn Yes. My name's Van Horn. I have an eleven o'clock appointment with Dr. Valentine.
Receptionist Please have a seat, Mr. Van Horn. The doctor will be with you in a minute.
Mr. Van Horn Thank you.

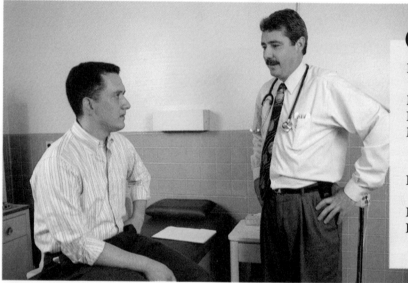

B

Dr. Valentine Well, Mr. Van Horn, what can I do for you?
Mr. Van Horn I don't feel very well.
Dr. Valentine What's the matter?
Mr. Van Horn I woke up with a terrible sore throat, and I've got a headache.
Dr. Valentine That's too bad. Do you have a fever?
Mr. Van Horn I don't know.
Dr. Valentine Well, let's take your temperature and find out.

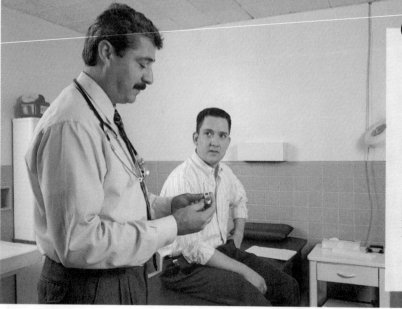

C

Dr. Valentine Well, it looks like you've got the flu. Nothing serious, but you shouldn't go to work. You should stay in bed for a few days and get some rest.
Mr. Van Horn What should I do for my headache?
Dr. Valentine You can take some aspirin. And try to drink lots of water or juice.
Mr. Van Horn O.K.
Dr. Valentine If you don't feel better in a couple of days, give me a call.

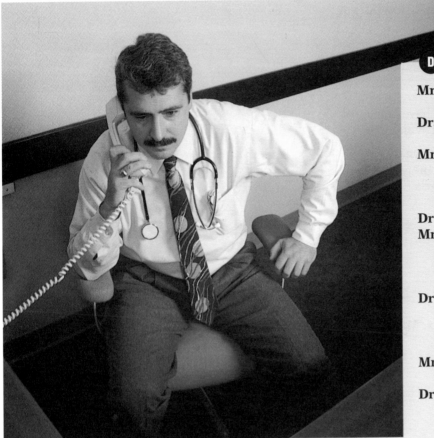

D

Mr. Van Horn Dr. Valentine? Dick Van Horn.

Dr. Valentine Yes, Mr. Van Horn. How do you feel today?

Mr. Van Horn My throat still hurts, but I feel a little better, thanks. But that's not why I'm calling.

Dr. Valentine Oh?

Mr. Van Horn Now my wife is sick. Her whole body hurts, so she can't get out of bed. What should I do?

Dr. Valentine Well, she probably has the flu, too, so she should take it easy and drink lots of liquids.

Mr. Van Horn Should I give her some aspirin?

Dr. Valentine Yes, it should help her aches and pains. I'm sure she'll be fine in a day or two.

Figure it out

1. Listen and say *True* or *False*.

1. Mr. Van Horn has the flu.
2. Mrs. Van Horn has the flu.
3. Dr. Valentine has the flu.

2. Listen again and complete the sentences with the words in the list.

1. I have an eleven o'clock _____ with Dr. Valentine.
2. Do you have a _____ ?
3. Well, let's take your _____ and find out.
4. You shouldn't go to work. You _____ stay in bed for a few days.
5. She _____ has the flu, too.

a. fever
b. probably
c. should
d. appointment
e. temperature

3. Find another way to say it.

1. Please sit down.   *Please have a seat.*
2. I feel sick.
3. What's wrong?
4. My head hurts.
5. I still have a sore throat.
6. She can't get out of bed because her whole body hurts.
7. Drink lots of water or juice.

8. What's the matter?

 1 ▶ **Put the lines of the conversation in order.**
▶ **Listen to check your answers.**

_____ Please have a seat, Mr. Van Horn. The doctor will be with you in a minute.
_____ Thank you.
__*1*_ May I help you?
_____ Yes. My name's Van Horn. I have an eleven o'clock appointment with Dr. Valentine.

▶ **Imagine you are in a doctor's office. Act out the conversation with a partner. Use your own last name, your doctor's name, and the actual time.**

2 ▶ **Listen to these statements. Match each problem with the picture it describes.**

_*g*_ 1. I've got a headache.
_____ 2. I have a cold.
_____ 3. I've got a sore throat.
_____ 4. I've got a toothache.
_____ 5. I have a fever.
_____ 6. I have a backache.
_____ 7. I've got a stomachache.
_____ 8. I've got the flu.

a   b   c

d   e   f   g   h

3 ▶ **Listen to the conversation.**
▶ **Imagine you have one of the problems in exercise 2 above. Act out the conversation with a partner.**

A I don't feel very well.
B What's wrong?
A I've got a headache.
B Oh, that's too bad.

Review: *Have got*	
I have **I've got**	a headache.

4 ▶ **Listen to the conversation. The man has six problems. What are they?**

1. *His feet hurt.*
2. _____
3. _____
4. _____
5. _____
6. _____

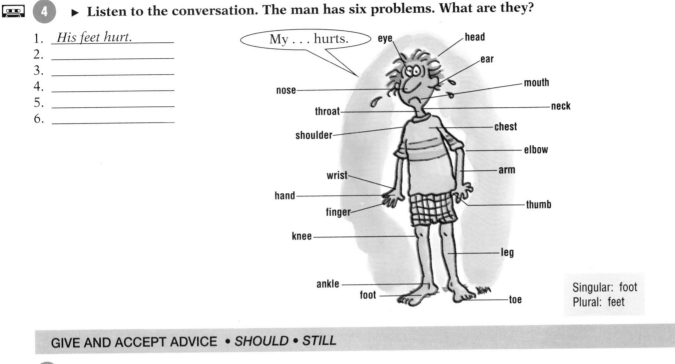

My . . . hurts.

eye • head • ear • mouth • neck • nose • throat • shoulder • chest • elbow • arm • wrist • hand • thumb • finger • knee • leg • ankle • foot • toe

Singular: foot
Plural: feet

GIVE AND ACCEPT ADVICE • *SHOULD* • *STILL*

5 ▶ **Listen to the two conversations.**
▶ **Imagine you've been sick. Work with a partner and act out the conversations. Use your own information.**

A How do you feel today?

B (I feel) awful.

B Much better, thanks.

A What's the matter?

B My throat still hurts.

A Maybe you should see a doctor.

B That's probably a good idea.

Some advice

Maybe you should	see a doctor. see a dentist. get some rest. stay in bed. take some aspirin. lie down.

Still

My throat **still** hurts.
I **still** have a sore throat.
I've **still** got a sore throat.

GIVE AND ACCEPT ADVICE • *SHOULD* • REVIEW: IMPERSONAL PRONOUN *YOU*

6 ▶ **Study the frames: *Should***

Information questions

What	should	I he they	do?

Statements

You He They	should shouldn't	call a doctor. go to work.

Yes-no questions

Should she stay in bed?

Short answers

Yes, she should. No, she shouldn't.

7 ▶ **Put the words in order to make questions.**
▶ **Discuss the questions in a group.**
▶ **Make a chart on the board, giving a remedy for each problem.**

1. should/What/do/you/for a headache?
2. drink liquids/Should/you/when you've got the flu?
3. What/for a sore throat/do/you/should?
4. you/take aspirin/for aches and pains/Should?
5. What/do/should/you/for a toothache?
6. for a stomachache/What/do/should/you?

9. Can you use a computer?

1
▶ Look at the pictures as you listen to what each person says.
▶ Tell your classmates which things you can and can't do.

I can type, but I can't use a computer.

1. type

2. use a computer

3. use a fax machine

4. file

5. take dictation

6. operate a copy machine

7. balance a checkbook

8. speak another language

2
▶ Dr. Clark is interviewing for a receptionist. Listen to the conversation and check (√) the things the applicant can do.

Applicant: *Daniel Russo*

Office Skills

____ type

____ use a computer

____ use a fax machine

____ file

____ operate a copy machine

____ balance a checkbook

Languages: *can only speak English*

Other: *can start in two weeks*

3 ▶ **Study the frames:** *Can*

Information questions			
What	can	you he she	do?
When		we they	start the job?

Statements		
I He She You They	can can't	type. start next week.

Yes-no questions	Short answers
Can you **use** a computer?	Yes, I **can.** No, I **can't.**

can't = cannot

4 ▶ **Here are three more people who are interviewing for the receptionist's job in Dr. Clark's office. Listen as they talk about themselves.**

Sylvia Brodsky

Alice Kwan

John Havock

What can I say about myself? I can't use a computer, but I can type and use other office machines—a copy machine or fax, for example. And my math is very good. Also, I can start immediately—tomorrow if you want—and I can work late when it's necessary. I guess that's all. I'd like to work in a doctor's office because I like to help people.

I'd like to have this job because it pays well. My office skills are excellent—I can use all office machines, and I can type 80 words a minute. Unfortunately, I can't help with the bookkeeping because my math is terrible. I can start in two weeks if that's O.K. Oh, and by the way, I studied nursing two years ago, but I didn't finish.

This is a surprise. I hate to go to the doctor, and here I am in a doctor's office. Anyway, I can use a computer and things. And I don't have a job, so I can start this week. What else? I can't balance my own checkbook, so I don't want to do any bookkeeping. But I can speak three languages. And oh, I can't work late very often because I play baseball every day after work.

▶ **Ask questions about each person.**

A Can Sylvia type?
B Yes, she can.
A Can she use a computer?
B . . .
A When can she start the job?
B . . .

5 ▶ **Which of the four applicants—Daniel Russo, Sylvia Brodsky, Alice Kwan, or John Havock—should the doctor hire? Work in a group and decide.**
▶ **Tell the class who your group chose and why.**

*The doctor should hire Sylvia **because** she can start immediately.*
*Sylvia can start immediately, **so** the doctor should hire her.*

10. I'm sorry I'm late.

Steve Kovacs's sister, Eva, is late for school this morning. Her first class is Chemistry with Miss Edwards.

1

Miss Edwards	Good morning, Eva.
Eva	Oh, Miss Edwards, I'm sorry I'm late.
Miss Edwards	That's all right. We just began. You look a little tired. Is anything wrong?
Eva	No, not really. I went to a soccer game last night because I wanted to take some pictures. Then I wanted to develop them right away, so I was up until midnight.
Miss Edwards	You should really get more sleep at night.
Eva	I know. I'm not going to do that again. Would you like to see my pictures?
Miss Edwards	I'd love to. But let's wait until after class, O.K.?
Eva	Oh, sure.
Miss Edwards	Do you think you can do today's experiment?
Eva	Yes. I went over it after school yesterday. Who should I work with?
Miss Edwards	Why don't you work with Bill?
Eva	O.K.

Eva	This is my brother, Steve. He played in the game last night.
Miss Edwards	Hmmm. You look like him.
Eva	Yeah. Everybody says that.

2. Figure it out

True or *False*? **Correct the false statements.**

1. Eva went to bed late last night. *True.*
2. Eva got to school early this morning.
3. Steve took some pictures of Eva at the soccer game.
4. Eva developed her own pictures.
5. Eva is going to do today's chemistry experiment with Bill.
6. Eva doesn't look like her brother.

The students are listening to an announcement over the loudspeaker. Read the questions below. Then listen to the announcements and answer them.

1. When's the football game?
2. How much are the tickets?
3. Where can the students buy tickets?

📼 **4. How to say it**

Practice the conversation.

A Can you answer the first question?
　[kən]

B No, I can't, but I can answer the second one.
　　[kænt]　　　　[kən]

A Good. Can someone answer the first question?
　　[kən]

C I can, Miss Edwards.
　　[kæn]

5. Your turn

Bobby Mendez, one of the students in Miss Edwards's class, isn't feeling well. He's talking to his friend Bonnie Perkins. Act out the conversation.

Bonnie _____ ?
Bobby I feel awful. I have a terrible headache.
Bonnie _____ .
Bobby The nurse isn't there. She doesn't come until 10 o'clock.
Bonnie _____ .
Bobby I don't have any aspirin.
Bonnie _____ .
Bobby That's a good idea. . . . Excuse me, Miss Edwards. Do you have any aspirin?

11.

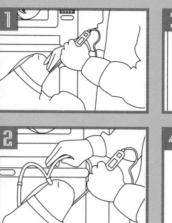
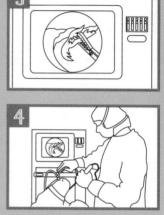

1. In video surgery, the doctor puts a small camera lens inside the knee.
2. The doctor inserts a tiny surgical instrument.

3. The lens sends pictures to a TV screen. 4. As he works, the doctor can see the inside of the knee and make accurate repairs.

Americans love sports — they love to play them, to watch them on television, and to talk about them. But this national pastime sometimes has serious consequences — at least for the players. People who play tennis year after year, for example, often develop "tennis elbow." And it is easy to hurt a knee or shoulder in a soccer or football game. These injuries happen while the player is having fun, but they still hurt.

A few months ago, Kathleen Simmons injured her knee in a volleyball game. Her doctor told her to rest her knee and wear a bandage. Simmons, a sports writer for a city newspaper, loves to play volleyball. When her doctor's advice did not work, she thought she would never play again.

Then Simmons learned about "video surgery." With the help of video technology, doctors can now repair many injuries and get people back on the playing field and back to their jobs much faster. Simmons found a hospital that was using this new technology and made an appointment. Doctors there told her the surgery could help.

For the operation, her doctor put a very small camera lens inside her knee. The special lens sent back pictures, which appeared on a television screen. The doctor then inserted a tiny surgical instrument. As he worked, he could see the inside of Kathleen's knee on the TV. With the help of the large picture on the screen, he was able to make very accurate repairs without opening her knee.

Simmons started walking five days after her operation. "My knee hurt a lot the first few days," she reported. "But I felt better very quickly." Now, six months after her operation, Simmons can do everything she did before her injury. "It feels like a new knee," she said. "I can even play volleyball again."

Kathleen Simmons playing volleyball after her operation

1. Choose the best title for the article.

    a. Sports in America   b. Video Surgery   c. Volleyball—A Dangerous Game?

2. Match the words with their synonyms. Use a dictionary if necessary.

1. pastime   a. very small
2. consequence   b. exact
3. injure   c. hurt
4. surgery   d. operation
5. accurate   e. result
6. tiny   f. leisure-time activity

FUNCTIONS/THEMES	LANGUAGE	FORMS
Ask what someone is doing	What are you looking for? A telephone. There's one right there. Who are you looking for? A waitress. I don't see one.	Review: the present continuous Verbs + prepositions
Offer help	I'll go and look for one. I'll go look for one.	*Go* and *come* with and without *and*
Talk about a problem	What's wrong? The phone isn't working. The elevator doesn't work.	Equivalent uses of the present continuous and simple present
Make a suggestion	Why don't you try again later? Let's go find another one.	
Make a telephone call	Hello. Could I speak to Cory, please? Who's calling? Lee Watson. Hold on, please.	
Get a wrong number	Could I speak to Cory, please? There's no one here by that name.	
Remind someone	I'm waiting for you at the theater. Did you forget our date?	

Preview the conversations.

This woman has a problem. What is it? What other things do you use that don't always work?

Did you ever forget something important—a meeting or an appointment? What happened?

12. The arrival

Nancy and David are reporters for a TV station. They're covering the arrival of a famous movie star this morning.

A

Nancy Where's Roger?

David He isn't here yet.

Nancy You're kidding! The plane's supposed to arrive in twenty minutes. We can't do this interview without him. It's important. We need pictures. Kim Bancroft is doing a new film here.

David He'll be here. He probably overslept again. . . . What are you looking for?

Nancy A telephone. We've got to call him.

David O.K. Let's go find one. I think they're down the hall.

B

David Why don't you try his house first? Then we can try the station.

Nancy O.K. (*Dials the number*) Oh, no!

David What's wrong?

Nancy This phone isn't working. It's making a funny noise. . . . Oh, wait . . . now the line's busy. . . . No. It doesn't work.

David Let's go find another one.

C

Nancy (*Dials the number*) Good. It's ringing.

Woman Hello?

Nancy Could I speak to Roger, please?

Woman There's no one here by that name. I think you have the wrong number.

Nancy Sorry. (*Hangs up*) I got the wrong number.

D

David O.K., let me try. (*Dials the number*) Then I'll call the station.

Roger Hello?

David Hello. Could I speak to Roger, please?

Roger This is Roger. Who's calling?

David This is David.

Roger Oh, hi, David. I didn't recognize your voice. What's up?

David What do you mean "What's up?" Nancy and I are at the airport. We're waiting for Kim Bancroft. Did you forget?

Roger Oh, no! What time is it?

David Ten to nine.

Roger I'm leaving right now. I'll be there as soon as I can.

Figure it out

1. Listen to the conversations and choose the correct answer.

a. Roger works at a TV station with Nancy and David.

b. Roger works at home.

2. Listen again and say *True* or *False*.

1. Roger is at the airport.   *False.*
2. Kim Bancroft's plane is going to arrive soon.
3. Nancy calls Roger and gets the wrong number.
4. David calls Roger and gets Roger's wife.
5. Roger is going to leave for the airport immediately.

3. Choose the correct response.

1. Where's Roger?
   a. He isn't here yet.
   b. Yes, he's here.

2. What are you looking for?
   a. We've got to call him.
   b. A telephone.

3. What's wrong?
   a. The line's busy.
   b. I'll try again.

4. Could I speak to Roger, please?
   a. There's no one here by that name.
   b. I got the wrong number.

4. Find another way to say it.

1. I don't believe it!   *You're kidding!*
2. We need him to do this interview.
3. He probably didn't get up on time again.
4. Why did you call?

13. I'm looking for . . .

1 ▶ Listen to five conversations. Who are the travelers looking for? Put a check (√) in the correct circles in the picture.

2 ▶ Listen to the two possible conversations.
▶ Look at the picture above and practice similar conversations with a partner.

A Who are you looking for?

B A waitress.

A There's one over there.　　　　**A** I don't see one.
B Oh, thanks.　　　　　　　　　　**B** I don't either.

3 ▶ Study the frame.

Review: Present continuous				
Who	**are**	you	**looking for?**	(**I'm looking for**) a waitress.
What	**is**	she	**listening to?**	(**She's listening to**) the weather.

Some verbs + prepositions		
look for	wait for	think about
listen to	look at	talk to

24 Unit 3

4 ▶ Complete each conversation with a question. Use a verb from the box in exercise 3.
▶ Listen to check your answers.

1. *What's she listening to?* — A Madonna cassette.
2. _____ — The receptionist at the hotel.
3. _____ — My wallet. I can't find it.
4. _____ — The ticket agent.

OFFER HELP • *GO* AND *COME* WITH AND WITHOUT *AND*

5 ▶ Listen to the two businessmen. First they go to the baggage carousel.
Where do they go next? Put the names of the places in order.

____ the bank
_1_ the baggage carousel
____ the taxi stand
____ the baggage carts
____ the telephones

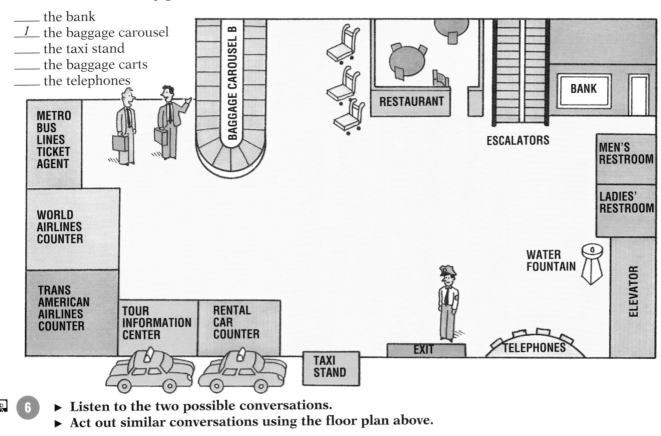

6 ▶ Listen to the two possible conversations.
▶ Act out similar conversations using the floor plan above.

A What are you looking for?

B A telephone.

A I'll go look for one. ⎯⎯ **A** There's one right there.

> You can join *go* and *come* to other verbs with or without *and*.
>
> I'll **go and look for** one. I'll **go look for** one.
> I'll **come and help** you. I'll **come help** you.

14. What's wrong?

 1 ► Listen to the conversations. Check (√) the things that are not working at the bus station.

2 ► Listen to the conversation.
► Look at the picture above and act out similar conversations with a partner.

A What's wrong?
B The coffee machine isn't working.
A Let's go find another one.
B O.K.

TALK ABOUT A PROBLEM • EQUIVALENT USES OF THE PRESENT CONTINUOUS AND SIMPLE PRESENT

3 ► Study the frame.

Equivalent uses of the present continuous and simple present		You can use the present continuous or the simple present to describe a recent change in condition or status.
The soda machine **works** now. The soda machine **is working** now.	I **live** in Los Angeles now. I'**m living** in Los Angeles now.	
The water fountain **doesn't work**. The water fountain **isn't working**.	I **don't work** at the bus station. I'**m not working** at the bus station.	

4 ► A woman is calling an old friend. Complete her conversation with the correct form of the verb in parentheses.
► Listen to check your work.

. . . I'm fine. . . . I _____ (call) from here in Dallas. . . . No, I _____ (live) in San Diego now, but I _____ (stay) at the Dallas Hilton for a conference. . . . My trip? It was O.K., but I think my suitcase fell off the bus. . . . No, I'm serious. My tape recorder _____ (not/record) anything, and my camera _____ (not/work). My hair dryer _____ (not/work) either, but maybe I can fix it. Enough about me. How are you? . . .

5 ► Talk to your classmates. Give an example of something that isn't working at home or at school.

My TV isn't working. My camera doesn't work either.

15. There's no one here by that name.

1 ▶ Complete the conversations with the suggestions in the box.
▶ Listen to check your work.
▶ Practice the conversations with a partner.

a. check the phone book   c. use my phone
b. try again later   d. try her house

2 ▶ Listen to the conversation.
▶ Practice the conversation in groups of four.

Man Hello?
Lee Hello. Could I speak to Cory, please?
Man There's no one here by that name.
Lee Sorry. (*Dials again*)
Woman Hello?
Lee Hello. Could I speak to Cory, please?
Woman Who's calling?
Lee Lee Watson.
Woman Hold on, please.
Cory Hi, Lee. What's up?
Lee We're waiting for you in our office. Did you forget our meeting?
Cory Oh, no! What time is it?
Lee It's ten to two.
Cory I'm leaving right now. I'll be there as soon as I can.

3 ▶ Work in groups of four. Look at the pictures and act out conversations similar to the one in exercise 2.

Did you forget our date?

Did you forget our game?

Did you forget your appointment?

I'll be there . . .

as soon as I can.
in half an hour.
in a few minutes.

16. You should get a job.

Bobby Mendez lives in the same apartment building as Eva Kovacs. He and Eva usually walk home from school together.

1

Eva	I've got to get a new camera.
Bobby	What's wrong with that one?
Eva	It just doesn't take very good pictures. I'd love to buy a new one, but they're so expensive.
Bobby	Why don't you get a job and earn some money?
Eva	Yeah, but where? It's hard to find a part-time job.
Bobby	I think Bonnie Perkins is working at Burger Ranch after school. Why don't you call her?
Eva	Yeah. That's a good idea—at least it's a start.
Bobby	Do you have her number?
Eva	No.
Bobby	Wait. I think I have it in my notebook. . . . Yeah, it's 555-2202.
Eva	Thanks. I'll call her later.

2. Figure it out

Answer *Eva, Bobby,* or *Bonnie*.

1. Who needs a new camera? *Eva.*
2. Who works at Burger Ranch?
3. Who wants to get a job after school?
4. Who looked for Bonnie's telephone number?
5. Who is going to call Bonnie about a job?

3. How to say it

Practice the phrases. Then practice the conversation.

got to	[gadə]	**A** I've got to get a camera.
got a	[gadə]	**B** You've already got a camera.
get a	[gedə]	**A** Yes, but I've got to get a new one.

4. Your turn

Rick Moore runs into Bobby and Eva on his way to a soccer game. Act out the conversation.

Bobby Hi, Rick. ———————————— ?
  Rick The number 28 bus stop. I can't find it.
Bobby ———————————————— .
  Rick Oh, yeah. I see it now.
Bobby ———————————————— ?
  Rick To the soccer game. Uh, what time is it now?
Bobby ———————————————— .
  Rick Quarter after three? Oh, no!
Bobby ———————————————— ?
  Rick The game starts in fifteen minutes.
Bobby No problem. Here comes the bus now.

5. Listen in

Read the questions below. Then listen to the conversation and answer the questions.

1. Who answered the phone when Eva called?
2. When does Bonnie work at Burger Ranch?
3. Are there jobs at Burger Ranch now?

17.

ELIZABETH TAYLOR
a legend of our time

Audiences fell in love with Elizabeth Taylor in 1944, when she starred in *National Velvet*—the story of Velvet Brown, a young girl who wins first place in a famous horse race. At first, the producers of the movie told Taylor that she was too small to play the part of Velvet. However, they waited for her for a few months as she exercised and dieted—and added three inches to her height in four months! Taylor was only twelve years old at the time, but she was already the determined professional people know today. Her performance in *National Velvet* is still considered the best by a child actress.

Elizabeth Taylor was born in London in 1932. Her parents, both Americans, had moved there for business reasons. When World War II started, the Taylors moved to Beverly Hills, California, and there Elizabeth started acting in movies. After her success as a child star, Taylor had no trouble moving into adult roles. She was nominated for an Academy Award five times between 1957 and 1966. She won twice for Best Actress: *Butterfield 8* (1960) and *Who's Afraid of Virginia Woolf?* (1966).

Taylor's fame and popularity gave her a lot of power with the movie studios, so she was able to demand very high fees for her movies. In 1963, she received $1 million for her part in *Cleopatra*—the highest fee received by any star up to that time.

Taylor's personal life has also been dramatic. She has been married eight times, most recently in 1991 to Larry Fortensky, a construction worker. Her third husband, Michael Todd, was killed in a plane crash while Taylor was making the movie *Cat on a Hot Tin Roof.* She finished the movie even though she had trouble talking because of her grief. Her fifth and sixth marriages, both to actor Richard Burton, had all the elements of modern romance, but they ended in divorce—twice. Taylor has also overcome serious illnesses—she nearly died of pneumonia twice—and she has been treated several times for alcohol and drug problems.

Elizabeth Taylor is a legend of our time. Like Velvet Brown in *National Velvet,* she has been lucky: she has beauty, talent, fame, and wealth. But she is also a hard worker. Taylor rarely acts in movies anymore. Instead, she puts her talent into her businesses—Elizabeth Taylor Perfumes have earned over $325 million—and into helping others—several years ago, she founded an organization that has raised more than $40 million for AIDS research and education.

Read the article. Then scan it for the number that completes each sentence.

1. Elizabeth Taylor was ＿＿ when she became a star.
2. She has been married ＿＿ times.
3. She has won ＿＿ Academy Awards.
4. She earned ＿＿ for *Cleopatra*.
5. Her perfumes have earned over ＿＿ .

FUNCTIONS/THEMES	LANGUAGE	FORMS
Shop for clothes Talk about location	I'm looking for a sweatshirt. They're over there, by the tank tops.	Prepositions of location: *in front of,* *in back of, by*
Talk about color and size	Any particular color? Yes. Navy blue. What size do you wear? A medium.	Colors and clothing sizes
Talk about fit	How do the shorts fit? They're not tight enough. They're too big.	*Too* and *enough*
Ask for an opinion	What do you think of this tank top? It seems a little tight.	Sense verbs + adjectives
Return something to a store	I'd like to return this tank top. Would you like to see a different style? No, I don't think so. Thanks.	
Compliment someone Talk about the past	Those sunglasses look good on you. Were they expensive? No, they weren't.	The past of *be*: Yes-no questions
Ask about store hours	How late are you open, please? Until 9:00.	
Identify items Talk about price	I like that chair. Which one? The striped one. How much does it cost? $349.99. It's on sale.	*Which* Indefinite pronouns *one* and *ones*

Preview the conversations.

Some stores in the United States are open every day of the week. Some are open late at night, too. When are stores usually open in your country?

Many stores in the United States have big sales two or three times a year. Prices are cheaper during sales. Do stores in your country have sales?

18. May I help you?

Harry's Sporting Goods is having a big sale, and Jack Sterling stops in to take a look.

A

Salesclerk May I help you?
Jack No, thanks. I'm just looking.
Uh . . . how late are you open?
Salesclerk Until 6:30.
Jack Thanks.

B

Salesclerk May I help you?
Jack I'm looking for a pair of exercise pants.
Salesclerk What size do you wear?
Jack A medium.
Salesclerk Any particular color?
Jack Do you have any in navy blue?
Salesclerk Yes, we do. . . . Here's a medium in navy blue.
Jack Where can I try them on?
Salesclerk The dressing rooms are right over there, by the swimsuits.

C

Salesclerk How do they fit?
Jack They're not big enough. The waist is too tight and the legs are too short. Let me try a large.
Salesclerk Certainly. Just a second.
Jack Oh, and you know that red tank top?
Salesclerk Which one? The one with the black stripes?
Jack Yes. How much does it cost?
Salesclerk $9.99. It's on sale. Would you like to try it on?
Jack Yes. In a medium.

D

Jack I bought these clothes today. What do you think?
Chris The pants look great on you. But the tank top seems a little small.
Jack Do you think so? Maybe I should return it for a larger size.
Chris The style is nice. Was it expensive?
Jack No. It was on sale.
Chris Let me try it on. Maybe it'll fit me. I love red.

Figure it out

1. Listen to the conversations. Then choose *a* or *b*.

1. a. Jack bought some exercise pants and a swimsuit.
   b. Jack bought some exercise pants and a tank top.

2. a. Chris likes Jack's new clothes.
   b. Chris doesn't like Jack's new clothes.

2. Listen again and say *True* or *False*.

1. The store closes at 6:30.   *True.*
2. Jack tries on two pairs of exercise pants.
3. Jack buys a navy blue tank top.
4. The tank top was expensive.
5. Chris is going to try on Jack's new tank top.

3. Match.

1. May I help you?
2. How late are you open?
3. What size do you wear?
4. How do they fit?
5. The tank top seems a little small.
6. Was it expensive?

a. No. It was on sale.
b. A medium.
c. Until 6:30.
d. No, thanks. I'm just looking.
e. Maybe I should return it for a larger size.
f. They're not big enough.

19. I need a sweatshirt.

▶ **Two young people are at Sports World.
Listen to their conversation and check (√)
the things they want to buy.**

2 ▶ **Listen to the conversation.**
▶ **Make a list of two things
that you want to buy. Then
act out the conversation
with a partner.**

A I need a sweatshirt.
B The sweatshirts are over there, by
the exercise pants. Are you
looking for any particular color?
A Oh, I don't know. Maybe gray or
navy blue.

by = near, next to

3
▸ **Look at the picture in exercise 1 and complete the conversations with** *in front of*, *in back of*, **and** *by*.
▸ **Listen to check your work. Can you use** *behind*, *across from*, *next to*, **and** *near* **in any of the sentences?**
▸ **Imagine you are in the store in exercise 1. Ask a salesperson where things are.**

in back of
(behind)

in front of

1. **A** I'm looking for some exercise pants.
   B They're _____ the shoes.
   A Thank you.

2. **A** Where are the socks?
   B They're _____ the gym bags.
   A Thanks a lot.

3. **A** Do you sell swimsuits?
   B Yes, we do. They're _____ the jackets.
   A Thanks.

4. **A** Do you sell exercise gloves?
   B Yes. They're _____ the cashier.
   A Great. Thanks.

5. **A** Where are the sweatshirts?
   B They're _____ the cashier.
   A Thanks.

6. **A** Where are the biking shorts?
   B They're _____ the T shirts.
   A Thank you.

4
▸ **Listen to the possible conversations.**
▸ **Imagine you are talking to a salesperson. Act out similar conversations with a partner.**

A May I help you?
B No, thanks. I'm just looking.

A May I help you?
B I'm looking for a sweatshirt.
A Any particular color?
B Yes. Navy blue.
A What size do you wear?
B A medium.
A Here's a medium in navy blue.
B Where can I try it on?
A The dressing rooms are over there, by the cashier.

a	sweatshirt cap jacket tank top T shirt	a pair of some	running shorts exercise pants sports gloves gym socks tennis shoes

Unisex sizes for men's and women's clothes

Extra Small (XS)
Small (S)
Medium (M)
Large (L)
Extra Large (XL)

See p. 166 for additional clothing and shoe sizes.

5
▸ **You are going to a friend's birthday party. Your friend loves to play tennis, goes to the gym three times a week, and goes to the beach every weekend. Work in a group and decide what gift to buy.**

20. How does the tank top fit?

1 ► **Listen to the conversation.**
Then circle the correct description.

1. The tank top is
   a. too small.
   b. not small enough.
   c. just right.

2. The shorts are
   a. too tight.
   b. not tight enough.
   c. just right.

3. The running shoes are
   a. too loose.
   b. not loose enough.
   c. just right.

4. The cap is
   a. too big.
   b. not big enough.
   c. just right.

too small = not big enough
too loose = not tight enough

cap

tank top

gloves

shorts

running shoes

2 ► **Listen to the possible conversations.**
► **Act out similar conversations about the clothes in exercise 1.**

A How does the tank top fit?

B It's just right.

B It's not big enough. Let me try a larger size.
A Certainly. Just a second.

large + er = larger
small + er = smaller

3 ► **Listen to the possible conversations.**
► **Imagine you are wearing something new today. Act out a similar conversation with a partner.**

A What do you think of this tank top?

B It looks great. How does it feel?

A It feels fine.

A It seems a little tight. Maybe I should return it for a larger size.

4 ► **Listen to the conversation.**
► **Practice the conversation with a partner.**
► **Act out similar conversations about the clothes in exercise 1.**

A I'd like to return this tank top.
B Would you like to see a different style?
A No, I don't think so. Thanks.

Sense verbs + adjectives		
It	looks	fine.
	feels	too tight.
They	seem	comfortable.

a different style?

another color?

a different size?

21. Was it expensive?

1 ▶ **Find the two conversations. Write *1* or *2* on each line.**
   ▶ **Listen to check your work.**

_1_ **A** Those sunglasses look good on you.
_2_ **A** That's a nice bag.

____ **B** Thanks. I bought them yesterday.
____ **B** Thanks. I bought it yesterday.

____ **A** It looks great. Was it expensive?
____ **A** They're great. Were they expensive?

____ **B** No. It was on sale.
____ **B** No. They were on sale.

▶ **Act out similar conversations
about the things in the pictures
or your own things.**

2 ▶ **Study the frames: The past of *be***

Yes-no questions

Were	you they	at school yesterday?
Was	he	
	it	expensive?

Short answers

Yes,	I	was.	No,	I	wasn't.
	they	were.		they	weren't.
	he it	was.		he it	wasn't.

3 ▶ **Complete the conversation with the past form of *be*.**
   ▶ **Listen to check your work.**

A _____ you at school yesterday?
B No, I _____ . Why?
A I _____ here either. I want to get the homework assignment.
B Where _____ you?
A I _____ at the eye doctor. I needed some new glasses.
B I thought those looked new. They look great on you. _____ they expensive?
A No. They _____ on sale. By the way, where _____ you yesterday?
B I _____ at the airport. My sister came home yesterday.
A Really? Where _____ she?
B In France. She _____ in a bicycle race.
A No kidding! _____ it a difficult race?
B Yes, it _____ . But she won!

4 ▶ **Imagine you were not at school yesterday. Answer your classmate's
questions. Explain where you were.**

22. Which one?

1 ▶ Listen to the conversation. Which store did the woman call? Circle the correct ad.

2 ▶ Listen to the two possible conversations.
▶ Look at the ad for Best Department Store. Which conversation is correct?
▶ Work with a partner. Act out a similar conversation about one of the other stores.

A Best Department Store. May I help you?
B Yes. How late are you open, please?
A Until 9:00.
B Are you open on Sunday?

A Yes, we are.	**A** No, we're not.
B O.K. Thank you.	**B** O.K. Thank you.
A You're welcome.	**A** You're welcome.

Martin's Furniture Store
Weekdays 10:00–6:00
Weekends 10:00–9:00

Grendel's Furniture
10AM–9PM Mon–Sat
Closed Sunday

Best Department Store
Open Seven Days
9:00– 9:00

Sports World
Monday – Saturday
10 AM – 8 PM

IDENTIFY ITEMS • *WHICH* • INDEFINITE PRONOUNS *ONE* AND *ONES*

3 ▶ A young couple is shopping for furniture. Listen to the conversation.
▶ Imagine you are shopping for furniture. Act out a similar conversation about the furniture in the picture.

A Look at that sofa.
B Which one?
A The plaid one.
B Oh, yeah. It's nice.

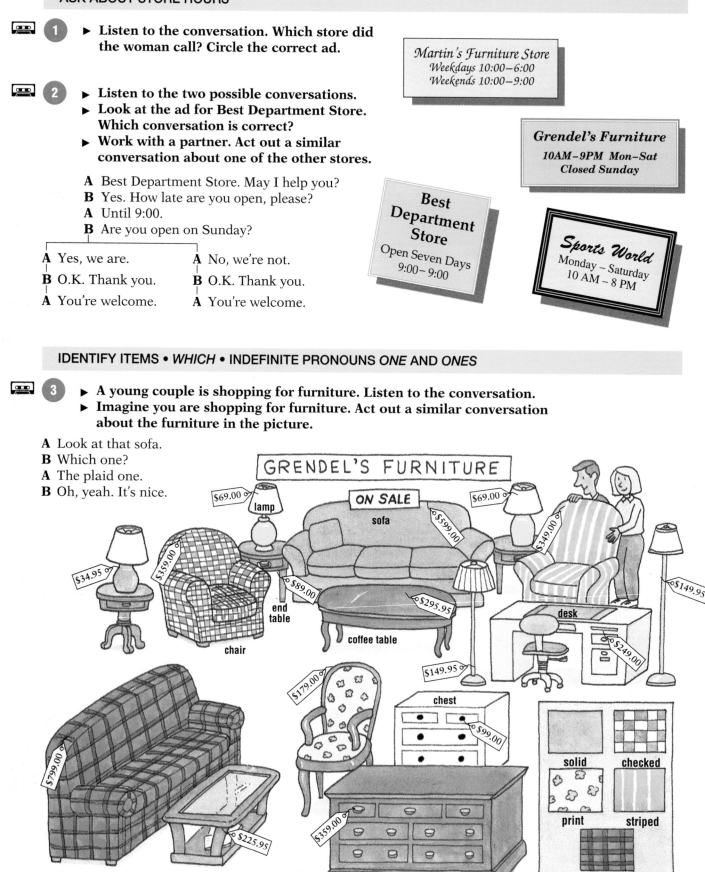

4 ▶ **Study the frame.**

Indefinite pronouns *one* and *ones*				
I like that chair.	Which **one**?	The striped **one**.	The **one** across from the sofa.	which one = which chair
I like those lamps.	Which **ones**?	The yellow **ones**.	The **ones** next to the table.	which ones = which lamps

5 ▶ **Complete the conversation with *one* or *ones*.**
   ▶ **Listen to check your work.**
   ▶ **Work with a partner and talk about the other pieces of furniture in exercise 3.**

A I like that chair.
B Which _____ ? The blue _____ ?
A No, the striped _____ .
   How much does it cost?
B $349.99. It's on sale.
A I like those lamps too.
B Which _____ ? The _____ by the desk?
A No. The _____ on the end tables.
   How much do they cost?
B $69.00 each.

6 ▶ **The couple is trying to decide where to put their new furniture. Put their conversation in order.**
   ▶ **Listen to check your work.**
   ▶ **Work with a partner and look at the picture. Which pieces of furniture are in the wrong place?**

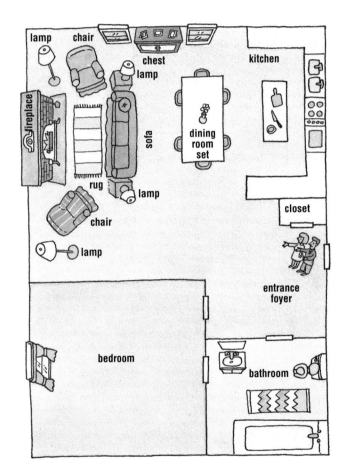

_1_ Let's put the sofa in front of the windows.
___ Let's put it in back of the sofa.
___ O.K. Where do you want the lamps?
___ No. Let's put it across from the fireplace.
___ Let's put them next to the sofa.
___ Which ones? The big ones?
___ Good idea. Now what about the chest?
___ No. The small ones.
_9_ Great.

7 ▶ **Work with a partner. Decide where to put the bedroom furniture.**

A *Let's put the chest in front of the window.*
B *Good idea. (No. Let's put it across from the bed instead.)*

23. It's up to you.

Olga Kurtz is the manager of the building where Eva Kovacs lives with her mother, Emma. Olga is showing an apartment to Tom Anderson, a pilot who just moved to Los Angeles.

1

Olga Well, here it is.

Tom Hmmm. It's nice, but it seems a little small. Do you have anything bigger?

Olga No. This is the only one available right now.

Tom Hmmm. I really have to find an apartment soon. I'm staying in a hotel right now.

Olga Well, this is a lot bigger than most one-bedroom apartments. The kitchen's big, there's a dining room, and there are five closets.

Tom Well, that's true.

Olga It's up to you. . . . By the way, the living room faces south. Look at all that sun.

Tom Yes, it's very bright. . . . Are the utilities included in the rent?

Olga No, you have to pay for gas and electricity yourself.

Tom How late can I call you? I'd like to think about it a little.

Olga I'll be in my office until six.

Tom Have you shown it to anyone else?

Olga A young couple looked at it this morning. They seemed very interested, but they haven't signed a lease yet.

Tom Well, I just don't know. But maybe I shouldn't take any chances. . . . All right. I think I'll take it.

Olga O.K. I'll need some references. What kind of work do you do?

Tom I'm a pilot with United American Airlines.

Olga Uh-huh. Well, why don't you come to my office and fill out the forms?

Tom Fine.

2. Figure it out

Say *True, False,* or *It doesn't say.*

1. Tom Anderson is looking for a small apartment. *False.*
2. He thinks the apartment is too small.
3. The rent is $600 a month.
4. Gas and electricity are included in the rent.
5. Some other people looked at the apartment today.
6. Tom is going to take the apartment.

3. Listen in

Olga Kurtz introduces Tom Anderson to Emma Kovacs. Read the questions below. Then listen to the conversation and answer the questions.

1. What's Tom's apartment number?
2. Where did Tom live before?
3. Do Tom and Emma live on the same floor?

🔊 4. How to say it

Practice the words and the conversation.

think	(θiŋk)
these	(ðiyz)
they	(ðey)
they're	(ðer)

A What do you think of these chairs?
B They seem a little small.
A They're on sale.
B No, they're too small.

$499.

5. Your turn

Tom is at a furniture store. He's looking for a new table and a set of chairs for his dining room. Act out the conversation.

Salesclerk	May I help you?
Tom	_____ .
Salesclerk	What do you think of this set?
Tom	_____ .
Salesclerk	You're right, it's big. But it's very nice, and it's on sale.
Tom	_____ ?
Salesclerk	$499.00.
Tom	_____ ?
Salesclerk	We're open until 9:00 tonight, so why don't you think about it?
Tom	_____ ?
Salesclerk	No. We're closed on Sunday.

Please Have A Seat

The chair is a relatively new item in the home. Up until the seventeenth century, it was used by royalty and the very rich as a status symbol, but few other people could afford much more than a wood stool or bench. Some people sat on cushions or just on the floor. Although chairs probably developed simultaneously in the East and the West, the western version has an interesting family tree.

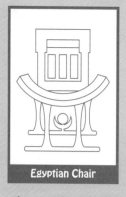

Egyptian Chair

The Egyptians, who built the first fine furniture 5,000 years ago, used chairs for two purposes. First, the king and other people in the royal household sat on thrones during public ceremonies and when they received visitors. Second, the wealthy used chairs for practical comfort in their homes. Many examples of ancient Egyptian chairs, from stools to a magnificent throne, were found in King Tut's tomb (1352 B.C.).

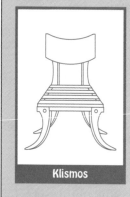

Klismos

Ancient Greek and Roman chairs (about 1100 B.C.–400 A.D.) developed from Egyptian styles. The most famous chair from this period was a Greek chair called a klismos—a simple but comfortable chair used in the home. Modern furniture designers still use the klismos style for dining room chairs. Roman chairs of the time were heavier and more elaborate than the Greek ones, and were often made with precious materials such as gold, silver, or ivory.

Throne

In the Middle Ages (400 A.D.–1300 A.D.), Europeans lost the art of making fine furniture. Only the richest people had more than one or two chairs in their homes. These chairs were often on a raised platform at one end of the room. Other people in the room sat below on stools or benches.

The greatest change in the use of the chair occurred in the seventeenth century. The new European middle class wanted comfortable furniture—with cloth and cushions—and chairs became common in every home, not just the homes of the nobility.

Louis XV Chair

Modern Chair

The greatest change in chair design occurred in our own century. With the use of plastics and metal, twentieth-century designers changed the shape of chairs radically for the first time since the ancient Egyptians.

1. Match to make sentences.

1. The ancient Egyptians
2. The ancient Greeks
3. In the Middle Ages, Europeans
4. The greatest change in furniture design

a. designed a style of chair that we still use.
b. built fine chairs 5,000 years ago.
c. occurred in the twentieth century.
d. lost the art of making fine furniture.

2. In a group, discuss this question.

Why do you think the leader of a business meeting is called the chairperson or "the chair"?

Review of units 1-4

1 ► Pat Russo has an interview for a job at a health club. Complete the receptionist's part of the conversation.

► Act out the conversation with a partner. Use your own name and the time.

Receptionist _____
     Pat Yes. My name is Pat Russo. I have a two o'clock appointment with Mr. Curtis.

Receptionist _____
     Pat Thank you.

2 ► Listen to Pat and another person talk about themselves. Check (√) *Yes* or *No* to complete the questionnaires.

► Work in a group. Who do you think should get the job?

Name Patricia Russo	**Date** March 15	
	Yes	No
Plays sports	——	——
Goes to a gym	——	——
Can use a computer	——	——
Understands bookkeeping	——	——
Speaks another language	——	——
Can start in two weeks	——	——
Can work weekends	——	——

Name Daniel Hall	**Date** March 15	
	Yes	No
Plays sports	——	——
Goes to a gym	——	——
Can use a computer	——	——
Understands bookkeeping	——	——
Speaks another language	——	——
Can start in two weeks	——	——
Can work weekends	——	——

3 ► Work in a group. What do you think Pat prefers to do in her free time? What do you think she doesn't like to do? What about Daniel? Use your imagination.

4 ► Pat is buying some clothes for her new job. Complete the conversation.

► Act out a similar conversation with a partner.

UNISEX SIZES XS–XL

$12.99 $12.99 $11.00 $11.00
$14.95 $14.95 $6.99 $6.99

Salesperson May I help you?
     Pat _____ .
Salesperson Which one? The dark green one?
     Pat _____ .
Salesperson Oh, the light green one. Certainly. What size do you wear?
     Pat _____ .
Salesperson Here's a medium in light green.
     Pat _____ ?
Salesperson $12.99. It's on sale.
     Pat _____ ?
Salesperson The dressing rooms are over there, by the swimsuits.

5 ▶ Imagine you are trying on one of these items.
Talk to the salesperson about the fit and ask for a different size.

 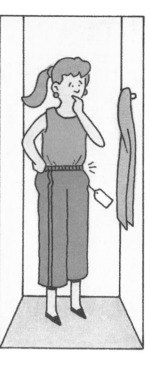  

6 ▶ Pat is talking to her neighbor Kim.
Complete the conversation with the past of *be*.
▶ Listen to check your answers.
▶ Work with a partner. Imagine you have a new job.
Act out a similar conversation, using your own information.

Kim Hi, Pat. _____ you at work today? I
called your office, but no one answered.

Pat No, I _____ . Yesterday _____ my last
day as a secretary. I'm starting a new job.

Kim Really? Where?

Pat At a health club. I'm going to be the
manager.

Kim That's great. So where _____ you today?

Pat My daughter and I _____ at the City
Shopping Center all afternoon. I needed
some clothes for my new job.

Kim Yeah. I can see you have a new tank top.
It looks good on you. _____ it expensive?

Pat No. It _____ on sale. These exercise
pants _____ on sale, too.

7 ▶ Listen to the radio ad for Pat's health
club. Then circle the name of the club.
▶ Work with a partner. Imagine you want
to know when one of the other clubs is
open. Call and find out.

POWER HOUSE *open*

Weekdays 8 A.M.–Midnight
Weekends 11 A.M.–10 P.M.
Stop by and see us. Your
first workout is FREE
555-3030

THE WORKOUT CENTER

Weekdays 7 A.M.–11 P.M.
Weekends 9 A.M.–9 P.M.
Call us at 555-5000 for
more information.

YMCA
Health Club

Weekdays 9 A.M.–9 P.M.
Weekends 10 A.M.–10 P.M.
Our Number is 555-2525

8 ▸ Listen to the rest of the ad for the health club in exercise 7. Then look at the brochure. Circle the things that are available.

9 ▸ Pat is meeting her co-workers for the first time. Complete Pat's part of the conversation.
 ▸ Imagine you are one of the people in the brochure. Act out the conversation with a partner.
 ▸ Act out a similar conversation, using your own names and information.

Dick Are you Patricia?
Pat _____
Dick I'm Richard, but everybody calls me Dick.
Pat _____
Dick Nice to meet you, too. So where do you live, Pat?
Pat _____
Dick I live here in Atlanta, too. On Fifteenth Street.

The perfect club for you!

swimming pool

workout room

tennis court

child care center

aerobics classes

racquetball court

Our Staff

Rose Lecrux
Receptionist
66 Peachtree Street
Atlanta, Georgia

Richard (Dick) Evans
Racquetball Instructor
15th Street
Atlanta, Georgia

Marcia (Marcy) Santiago
Aerobics Instructor
41 Bear Lane
Atlanta, Georgia

Carl Lee
Swimming Instructor
Butler Street
Atlanta, Georgia

10 ▸ Work in groups of three. Imagine you are the receptionist at a health club. One of your classmates is the new manager, and one is an instructor. Introduce the new manager and the instructor.

11A ▸ Student A follows the instructions below.
 Student B follows the instructions on page 46.

Student A   Imagine you are standing near the receptionist's desk at The Workout Center. Ask your partner for the location of the *men's or women's dressing room*, the *racquetball court*, the *telephones*, and the *sandwich machine*. Label all the places your partner can find on the floor plan. Then answer your partner's questions.

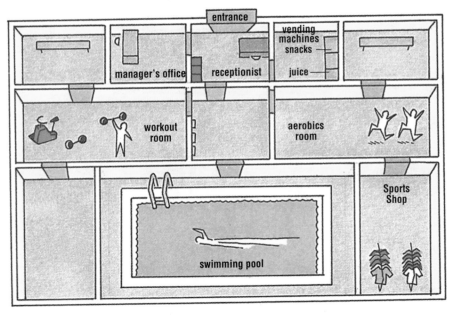

entrance

vending machines
snacks
juice

manager's office   receptionist

workout room

aerobics room

Sports Shop

swimming pool

11B ► Student B follows the instructions below.
Student A follows the instructions on page 45.

Student B Imagine you are standing near the receptionist's desk at The Workout Center. Answer your partner's questions. Then ask your partner for the location of the *workout room*, the *Sports Shop*, the *manager's office*, and the *aerobics room*. Label all the places your partner can find on the floor plan.

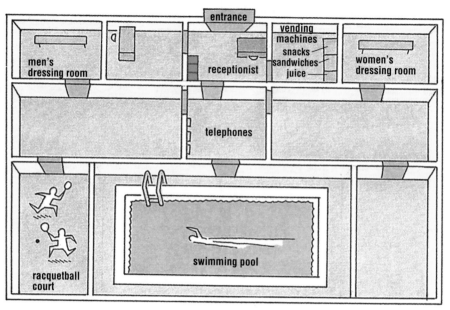

12 ► Listen to the conversation between the receptionist and one of the instructors. Check (√) the things that aren't working.

► Work with a partner. Imagine you are in the health club and have one of these problems. State the problem and make a suggestion.

13 ► Complete Dick's part of the conversation.

► Imagine you are in the gym and have a problem. Act out a similar conversation.

A What's the matter?
B _____
A Maybe you should see a doctor.
B _____

PREVIEW

FUNCTIONS/THEMES	LANGUAGE	FORMS
Give instructions	Put the document you want to send here. Don't put newspaper into the machine.	The affirmative and negative imperative Preposition *into*
Talk about future plans	When are you going to go to Montreal? In the winter. Are you going to go out? Yeah. I'm going to go shopping.	The future with *going to*
Talk about the seasons and the weather	What's the weather like in the winter? It's cold and snowy, so I'm going to go skiing. What's it like out? It's snowing.	The seasons and the weather
Invite someone informally Give an excuse	Do you want to come along? I'd like to, but I have to wait for a phone call.	

Preview the conversations.

Some parts of the United States have four seasons—spring, summer, fall, and winter. In the northern states, for example, it rains in the spring, it's hot in the summer, it's cool in the fall, and it's cold and snowy in the winter. What are the seasons in your country?

These days a lot of offices have answering machines, fax machines, and copy machines. Sometimes there is even a coffee machine or vending machines for the employees. What machines are common in offices in your country?

25. How does it work?

 Linda Cheng and Jerry Rothman own Holiday Tours, a small travel agency. Jerry is late this morning.

A

Linda Jerry! Where were you?

Jerry Am I late? Sorry. I wanted to buy a couple of things for the office on my way to work.

Linda What did you buy?

Jerry A new telephone answering machine.

Linda Oh, great! Let's see. (*Jerry takes the machine out of the box.*) How does it work?

Jerry Let me plug it in and I'll show you.

Linda Hey, don't plug it in with wet hands. Let me do it.

Jerry Oh, O.K.

Linda And should I connect it to the phone line?

Jerry Yeah. Now just turn this dial to ANSWER. Then push the ON button.

Linda Hmmm. Nice. That's a lot easier than our old one.

B

Linda And what's that?

Jerry A coffee maker. Look. (*He takes it out of the box.*) You just put the coffee in here, the water in here, and then turn on the machine.

Linda Not bad. Where did you get it?

Jerry That little store on the corner. They're having a spring sale.

Linda Well, let's try it out. Where's the coffee?

Jerry I forgot to get some. I'll get it at lunchtime.

C

Linda What's it like out? Still raining?
Jerry No, it stopped. Why? Are you going to go out?
Linda Later. I'm going to have lunch with a client. Do you want to come along?
Jerry Where are you planning to go?
Linda We'll probably just get a sandwich somewhere. Nothing special.
Jerry I don't know. I'll let you know around lunchtime.

D

Linda So, what did you decide? Are you going to join us?
Jerry No, I don't think so. I'm just going to go get a sandwich and eat at my desk.
Linda O.K. See you later. And, Jerry? Don't forget to turn on the answering machine when you go out.
Jerry I won't. And I'll pick up some coffee.

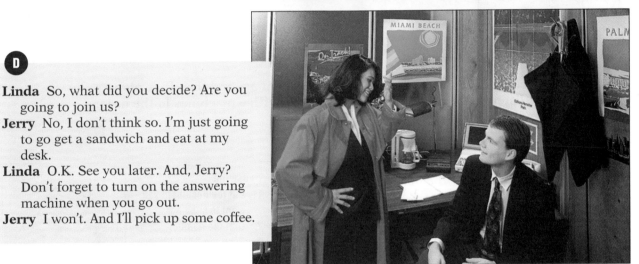

Figure it out

1. Listen to the conversations. Say *True* or *False*.

1. Jerry was late for work.
2. Linda bought some things for the office.
3. Jerry's going to have lunch with Linda.

2. Listen again and choose the correct response.

1. Where were you?
   a. What did you buy?
   b. Am I late? Sorry.

2. How does it work?
   a. Just turn this dial to ANSWER. Then push the ON button.
   b. It's a telephone answering machine.

3. What's that?
   a. That little store on the corner.
   b. A coffee maker.

4. Where's the coffee?
   a. You just put the coffee in here.
   b. I forgot to get some.

5. What's it like out? Still raining?
   a. No, it stopped.
   b. Oh, that's too bad.

6. Are you going to join us?
   a. See you later.
   b. No, I don't think so.

7. Don't forget to turn on the answering machine.
   a. I won't.
   b. I'll get some at lunchtime.

26. Push the ON button.

1 ▶ An office manager is showing a new travel agent around the office above. As you listen to the conversation, number the office machines in the order they mention them.

2 ▶ Complete each instruction card with the name of one of the machines in the box.
▶ Listen to the instructions and check your work.

a. computer
b. VCR
c. telephone answering machine
d. copy machine
e. fax machine
f. cassette player

To use the _____ :
1. Put the document you want to copy here.
2. Push the PRINT button.
3. DO NOT use paper clips or staples near the machine.

To use the _____ :
1. Put the document you want to send here.
2. Dial the number.
3. Push the START button.
4. DON'T put newspaper* into the machine.
*newspaper is too thin

To use the _____ :
1. Connect the machine to your phone line and turn the dial to ANSWER.
2. Push the ON button.
3. DO NOT put anything on the machine.

3 ▶ Listen to the conversation.
▶ Practice the conversation with a partner.
▶ Act out a similar conversation, asking about one of the office machines in exercise 1.

A How does the fax machine work?
B Put the document you want to send here and then dial the telephone number. Then you push the START button. And by the way, don't put newspaper into the machine.
A O.K. That's easy enough. Thanks.

Prepositions *in* and *into*

Don't put newspaper **in** the machine.
Don't put newspaper **in**.
Don't put newspaper **into** the machine.

Into means the same as *in*. However, an object always follows *into*.

4 ▶ **Study the frames.**

Affirmative imperative	Negative imperative	Use impersonal *you* to soften an instruction.
Put the document here.	**Do not (Don't) put** newspaper in the fax machine.	**You put** the document here. **You don't put** the document there.

5 ▶ **Complete the instructions for using a VCR with the imperative form.**
▶ **Listen to check your work.**

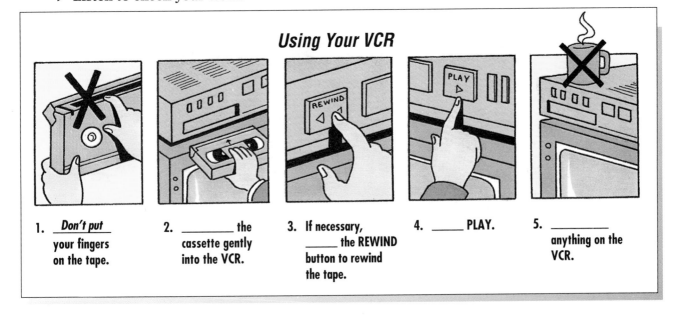

Using Your VCR

1. *Don't put* your fingers on the tape.
2. _____ the cassette gently into the VCR.
3. If necessary, _____ the REWIND button to rewind the tape.
4. _____ PLAY.
5. _____ anything on the VCR.

6 ▶ **Work with a partner. Explain how to use a cassette player.**

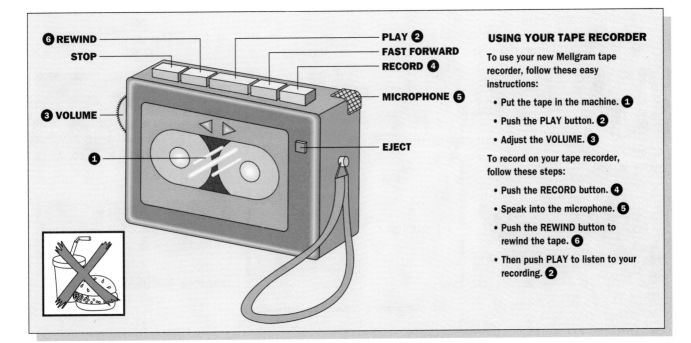

USING YOUR TAPE RECORDER

To use your new Mellgram tape recorder, follow these easy instructions:

- Put the tape in the machine. **1**
- Push the PLAY button. **2**
- Adjust the VOLUME. **3**

To record on your tape recorder, follow these steps:

- Push the RECORD button. **4**
- Speak into the microphone. **5**
- Push the REWIND button to rewind the tape. **6**
- Then push PLAY to listen to your recording. **2**

27. When are you going to go to Montreal?

1 ▶ Look at the three travel brochures below. Then listen to three radio ads. Write the name of the city each radio ad describes.

First radio ad: _____

Second radio ad: _____

Third radio ad: _____

2 ▶ Listen to the conversation.

▶ Practice the conversation with a partner.

▶ Imagine you're going to go to Montreal. Work with a partner and act out a similar conversation. Talk about a different season.

A So, what did you decide? When are you going to go to Montreal?

B (Probably) in the winter.

A What's the weather like in the winter?

B It's cold and snowy, so I'm going to go skiing.

It's...		
cold	cloudy	awful
cool	windy	terrible
warm	sunny	nice
hot	humid	beautiful

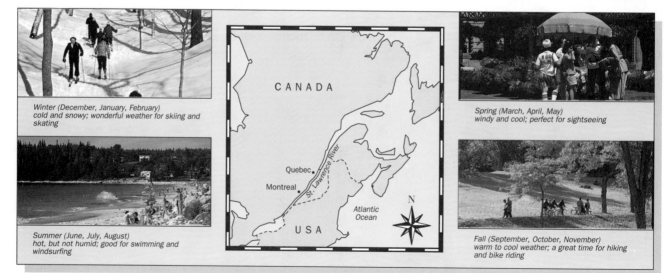

Winter (December, January, February)
cold and snowy; wonderful weather for skiing and skating

Summer (June, July, August)
hot, but not humid; good for swimming and windsurfing

Spring (March, April, May)
windy and cool; perfect for sightseeing

Fall (September, October, November)
warm to cool weather; a great time for hiking and bike riding

3 ▶ **Study the frames: The future with *going to***

Information questions					
When	**are**	you they	**going to**	**go**	to Montreal?
	is	she			

Affirmative statements			
I'm They're She's	**going to**	**go**	in the winter.

Negative statements		
I'm **not** They **aren't** She **isn't**	**going to**	**go**.

Yes-no questions				
Are	you they	**going to**	**stay**	in a hotel?
Is	she			

Short answers				
Yes,	I **am**. they **are**. she **is**.	No,	I'm **not**. they **aren't**. she **isn't**.	

Going to go is often reduced to *going*.

When are you **going** to Montreal?

4 ▶ **What did the traveler decide? Listen and check (√) the information.**

_____ **Tour to Montreal** _____

Hotels ****The Royal ___   ***The Hilton ___   **The Family Inn ✓

Meal Plans American Plan ___   Continental Plan ___
(breakfast and dinner)   (breakfast only)

Transportation   Air ___   Train ___   Bus ___
First Class ___
Business Class ___
Economy ___

Activities
Sports   **Tours**
___ skiing   ___ Shopping Adventure
___ skating   ___ Montreal by Night (Nightclubs)
___ windsurfing   ___ City Sightseeing
___ bike riding   ___ St. Lawrence River Cruise
___ hiking

5 ▶ **Work with a group. Decide where to go on vacation this year. You can choose one of the places in exercise 1 or any other place you prefer. Complete the chart.**
▶ **Tell the class about your plans.**

Some things to decide

Where and when are you going to go?
How are you going to get there?
Are you going to stay in a hotel or with friends?
What are you going to do there?

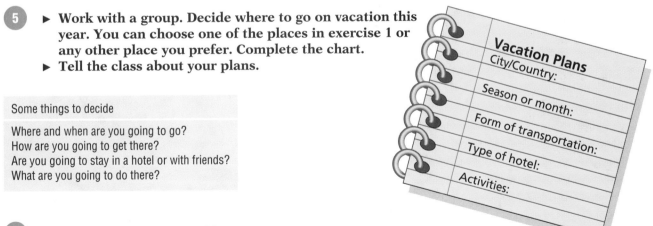

Vacation Plans
City/Country:
Season or month:
Form of transportation:
Type of hotel:
Activities:

6 ▶ **Listen to the two possible conversations.**
▶ **Imagine you are on vacation at the place you chose in exercise 5. Work with someone from your group and act out a similar conversation.**

A What's it like out?

B It's nice. Why? Are you going to go out?

A Yeah. I'm going to go shopping. Do you want to come along?

B Sure.   **B** I'd like to, but I have to wait for a phone call.

Some excuses

I have to wait for a phone call.
I have other plans.
I'm too tired.
I'm going to go skiing.

28. We can fix it.

Charley has stopped by Steve's shop after work.

1

Steve   Hi, Charley. How's it going at the bank?

Charley   Not too bad, I guess. A little boring. Hey, are you going home soon?

Steve   Pretty soon. I have a few more things to do. But I'll be ready in about ten minutes.

Charley   O.K. I'll wait. . . . Uh, what's the cassette player for?

Steve   I wrote a radio commercial for the shop, and I just taped it. Margaret and Bob helped me. Do you want to hear it?

Charley   You mean you're going to have an ad on the radio?

Steve   Yeah. I'm going to give this tape to an ad agency. Just as an idea. They can make a really professional ad from it.

Charley   That's a great idea. I bet you'll get a lot of new customers that way.

Steve   Boy, I hope so. I've got a lot of bills to pay.

Charley   I suppose this business is a big responsibility for you. But at least you like what you do.

Steve   Yes, I guess I do. O.K., so listen to this ad and tell me what you think. I think you'll like it. (*Turns on cassette player*)

Margaret's Voice   What's wrong, honey?

Bob's Voice   I don't know . . .

2. Figure it out

Say *True, False,* or *It doesn't say.*

1. Steve has a cassette player in his office.   *True.*
2. Charley's job at the bank isn't very interesting.
3. Charley wrote an ad for Steve's shop.
4. Steve wants to get more customers.
5. Charley doesn't have many bills to pay.
6. Steve likes his job.

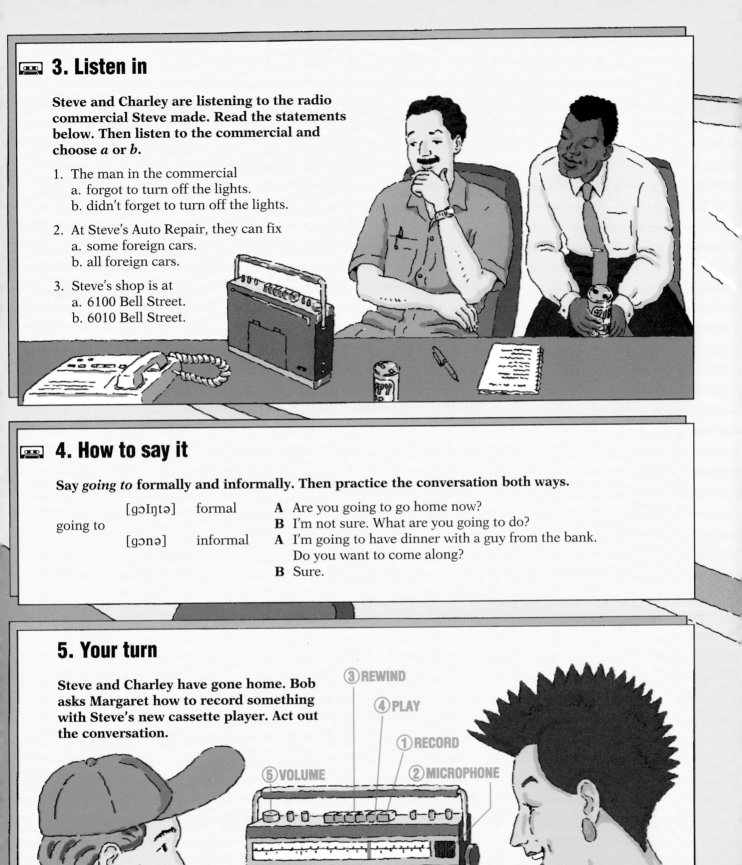

📼 3. Listen in

Steve and Charley are listening to the radio commercial Steve made. Read the statements below. Then listen to the commercial and choose *a* or *b*.

1. The man in the commercial
   a. forgot to turn off the lights.
   b. didn't forget to turn off the lights.

2. At Steve's Auto Repair, they can fix
   a. some foreign cars.
   b. all foreign cars.

3. Steve's shop is at
   a. 6100 Bell Street.
   b. 6010 Bell Street.

📼 4. How to say it

Say *going to* formally and informally. Then practice the conversation both ways.

going to   [gɔɪŋtə]   formal

A Are you going to go home now?
B I'm not sure. What are you going to do?

[gɔnə]   informal

A I'm going to have dinner with a guy from the bank. Do you want to come along?
B Sure.

5. Your turn

Steve and Charley have gone home. Bob asks Margaret how to record something with Steve's new cassette player. Act out the conversation.

③ REWIND
④ PLAY
① RECORD
② MICROPHONE
⑤ VOLUME

29.

What's Up with the Weather?

In recent years, the daily weather reports have sounded like real news—surprising and sometimes even frightening.
Examples:
- In the United States, a June snowfall in Colorado and floods in the southern California desert
- The worst drought in fifty years in a large part of the African continent
- The coldest summer in history in Melbourne, Australia

So, what's up with the weather? Are we seeing a worldwide change in climate, or are snowy summer days not really that strange? Scientists say that unusual weather is not really unusual at all. In fact, they say we should always expect extreme hot and cold or wet and dry periods. Scientists also point out that natural disasters can cause extreme weather that lasts for months or even years. Volcanic eruptions, for example, can change temperatures around the world. Other experts, however, point out that these explanations do not explain some major changes in the earth's climate—such as the rapid growth of the Sahara Desert during the last ten years.

The map below shows some of the strange weather in recent years, and some theories about what might be causing it.

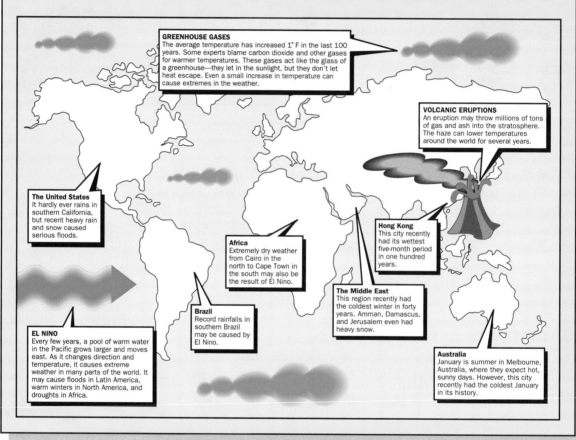

GREENHOUSE GASES
The average temperature has increased 1° F in the last 100 years. Some experts blame carbon dioxide and other gases for warmer temperatures. These gases act like the glass of a greenhouse—they let in the sunlight, but they don't let heat escape. Even a small increase in temperature can cause extremes in the weather.

VOLCANIC ERUPTIONS
An eruption may throw millions of tons of gas and ash into the stratosphere. The haze can lower temperatures around the world for several years.

The United States
It hardly ever rains in southern California, but recent heavy rain and snow caused serious floods.

Africa
Extremely dry weather from Cairo in the north to Cape Town in the south may also be the result of El Nino.

Hong Kong
This city recently had its wettest five-month period in one hundred years.

The Middle East
This region recently had the coldest winter in forty years. Amman, Damascus, and Jerusalem even had heavy snow.

Brazil
Record rainfalls in southern Brazil may be caused by El Nino.

EL NINO
Every few years, a pool of warm water in the Pacific grows larger and moves east. As it changes direction and temperature, it causes extreme weather in many parts of the world. It may cause floods in Latin America, warm winters in North America, and droughts in Africa.

Australia
January is summer in Melbourne, Australia, where they expect hot, sunny days. However, this city recently had the coldest January in its history.

1. Look at the map and find a place where recently the weather was unusually. . .

1. cold   _____
2. dry   _____
3. wet   _____

2. Match to make sentences.

1. El Nino
2. Greenhouse gases
3. Volcanic eruptions

    a. may cause lower temperatures.
    b. may cause droughts in Africa.
    c. may cause high temperatures.

3. Find the approximate location of your country on the map. Was it unusually wet or dry or hot or cold this year?

PREVIEW

FUNCTIONS/THEMES	LANGUAGE	FORMS
Order food in a restaurant	May I take your order? We need a few more minutes. Yes. I'd like a turkey sandwich, please.	
Ask for something	Could you bring us some water? Certainly. Do you need anything else? We don't have any forks.	*A, some,* and *any* with count and mass nouns
Ask for help informally	Could you help me with my homework? Sorry, I can't right now. I'm busy.	
Talk about possession	Whose briefcase is this? It's mine. It's my briefcase.	*Whose* Review: possessive pronouns and possessive adjectives

Preview the conversations.

There are a lot of inexpensive restaurants in the U.S. This family is having dinner at one of them.
Do people eat out often in your country? What kind of restaurants do they go to?

30. Eating out

 The Pearson family is eating in a restaurant, and Jim Phillips is their waiter.

A

Jim Hi. May I take your order?
Mr. Pearson We need a few more minutes.
Jim O.K. Take your time. I'll come back.

B

Jim Are you ready to order?
Mrs. Pearson Yes, I think so. I'd like the fried chicken, please.
Jim Would you like french fries or a baked potato with that?
Mrs. Pearson Umm . . . a baked potato.
Jim Soup or a salad?
Mrs. Pearson What kind of soup do you have?
Jim Vegetable.
Mrs. Pearson I'll have soup.
Jim Anything to drink?
Mrs. Pearson Coffee, I guess.
Daughter And I'll have a roast beef sandwich with french fries and a large soda.
Jim O.K. Would you like some soup or a salad to begin?
Daughter No, thanks.
Jim And what about you, sir?
Mr. Pearson I'll have the fried chicken, too. With a baked potato and a salad.
Jim To drink?
Mr. Pearson Just water. In fact, bring water for everyone.
Jim All right. I'll be back with your drinks in just a minute.

C

Mr. Pearson Excuse me.
Jim Yes? What can I get you?
Mr. Pearson We don't have any napkins.
Jim Oh, I'm sorry. I'll go get some. Do you need anything else?
Mr. Pearson Could you bring us some ketchup? This bottle is empty.
Mrs. Pearson And some more water.
Jim Certainly.

D

Jim Oh, Sandy, could you help me for a second?

Sandy Sorry, Jim, I can't right now. I'm busy. But maybe Carmen can.

Jim Hey, Carmen, could you help me with that table over there?

Carmen Sure. What do you need?

Jim Could you give them some napkins and some water? And a bottle of ketchup? I'd really appreciate it.

Carmen No problem.

E

Carmen Uh-oh. Whose briefcase is this? Somebody left it under the table.

Sandy It probably belongs to that couple at the cashier. This was their table.

Carmen I'll go ask. . . . Uh, excuse me. Whose briefcase is this?

Woman Oh, that's mine. Thank you very much.

Carmen You're welcome.

Figure it out

1. Listen to the conversations and choose *a* or *b*.

1. A family is having _____ in a restaurant.
   a. breakfast
   b. dinner

2. The waiter forgets to give the family
   a. napkins.
   b. menus.

3. Some people at another table forgot _____ when they left.
   a. a briefcase
   b. a handbag

2. Listen again and match.

1. May I take your order (Are you ready to order)?
2. I'd like the fried chicken, please.
3. What kind of soup do you have?
4. Anything to drink?
5. Excuse me.
6. Could you bring us some ketchup?
7. Whose briefcase is this?

a. Certainly.
b. Vegetable.
c. Coffee, I guess.
d. We need a few more minutes.
e. Yes? What can I get you?
f. Oh, that's mine.
g. Would you like french fries or a baked potato with that?

31. May I take your order?

1
- ▶ **Listen to the conversation.**
- ▶ **Practice the conversation with a partner.**

A May I take your order?
B We need a few more minutes.
A O.K. Take your time. I'll come back.

Home Trail Restaurant

$1.50

Soups
Vegetable   Chicken noodle

From Our Grill
Hamburger $2.95
Cheeseburger $3.95
    Served with french fries or cole slaw

Sandwiches
Tuna $2.50
Roast beef $3.95
Turkey $2.95
    Served with french fries or cole slaw

Desserts   **Beverages**
Chocolate cake $2.00   Coffee or tea $0.50
Apple pie $1.50   Soda small $0.50
                             large $0.75

```
         Dinner Specials
                               9.95
Roast beef                     7.50
Half chicken                   8.95
Fried fish
All dinner specials include french fries or
baked potato, soup or salad, and a beverage
```

Pasta House

Pasta
Spaghetti with meat sauce
Spaghetti with tomato sauce $6.95
Lasagna $4.95
Ravioli $7.00
                                     $6.25
(includes garlic bread and a salad)

Salads
Sliced tomatoes
Tossed salad $2.00
                                     $2.50

Desserts
Ice cream $1.50   **Beverages**
Vanilla   Coffee or Tea
Chocolate   Glass of wine $0.50
Fresh fruit $2.00   Soda $1.50
                                        $0.75

2
- ▶ **Listen to the people order. Then check (√) the menu the people are ordering from.**
- ▶ **Listen to the conversation again and circle the food the people order.**

3 ▶ **Listen to the conversation.**
▶ **Practice the conversation in groups of three.**

A Are you ready to order?
B Yes. I'd like a turkey sandwich, please.
A Would you like french fries or cole slaw with that?
B Cole slaw, please. And a cup of tea.
A And what about you, sir?
C I'll have the roast beef.
A How do you like your roast beef?
C Medium, please.
A O.K. Would you like french fries or a baked potato?
C I'll have a baked potato.
A Soup or salad to begin?
C I'll have chicken noodle soup.
A Anything to drink?
C Umm . . . a small diet soda.

Use *a* to order hamburgers and sandwiches, but *the* to order dinner.

I'll have **a** roast beef sandwich.
I'll have **the** roast beef.

Some ways to order meat

rare   medium   well done

4 ▶ **Work in groups of three. Imagine you are going out to dinner. Agree on one of the restaurants in exercise 2.**
▶ **Order dinner in the restaurant you chose. One person plays the role of the waiter, and the other two order from the menu. Then switch roles. Take turns being the waiter.**

5 ▶ **Listen to the two possible conversations.**
▶ **Imagine you are ordering dessert in a restaurant. Work in groups of three and act out similar conversations.**

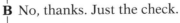
A Would you like some dessert?

B What do you have?
A We have chocolate cake and apple pie.
B I'll have apple pie.
A And you, sir?
C No, nothing for me.

B No, thanks. Just the check.
A Certainly.

32. Do you need anything else?

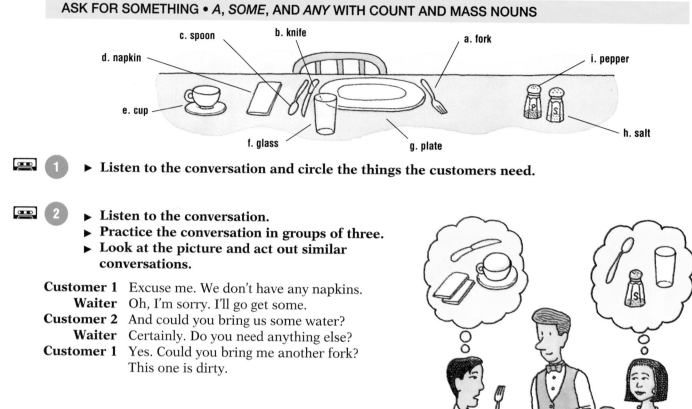

c. spoon b. knife a. fork i. pepper d. napkin e. cup f. glass g. plate h. salt

1 ▶ Listen to the conversation and circle the things the customers need.

2 ▶ Listen to the conversation.
▶ Practice the conversation in groups of three.
▶ Look at the picture and act out similar conversations.

Customer 1 Excuse me. We don't have any napkins.
Waiter Oh, I'm sorry. I'll go get some.
Customer 2 And could you bring us some water?
Waiter Certainly. Do you need anything else?
Customer 1 Yes. Could you bring me another fork? This one is dirty.

Use *a* or *some* when you ask for something you don't have.
Could you bring me **a** fork and **some** water?

Use *another* or *some more* when you need something you already have.
Could you bring me **another** fork? This one is dirty.

3 ▶ Study the frames: *A, some,* and *any* with count and mass nouns

Could you bring me (us)	**a**	fork?
	some	napkins? water?
Do you have	**any**	forks? ketchup?

| We (I) don't have | **any** | forks. napkins. water. ketchup. |

Count nouns have both singular and plural forms.
| fork | forks |
| napkin | napkins |

Mass nouns have one form.
salt   coffee   water

4 ▶ Complete the restaurant review with *a, some,* or *any*.

Last Saturday we tried Home Trail, _____ new restaurant on Ocean Drive. I had _____ roast beef sandwich and my friend had the chicken dinner. The food was delicious, but the service was _____ problem. It was slow, there weren't _____ forks or spoons on our table, and the waiter didn't bring _____ water until we asked. When we asked for more coffee, it simply never arrived. We got tired of asking for everything ("Could you bring me _____ napkin?" and "Do you have _____ salt?"). As I said, the food is good, but try Home Trail for dinner when you have a lot of time and patience.

5 ▶ Work in groups. Tell your group about a restaurant you went to that you didn't like.

33. Could you help me with this table?

ASK FOR HELP INFORMALLY

1
- ▶ Look at the pictures and complete the requests with a phrase from the box.
- ▶ Listen to check your work.
- ▶ Work with a partner. Ask for help with something.

a. this table
b. my coat
c. my homework
d. this check

> Could you help me with _____ ?

> Sorry, I can't right now. I'm busy.

> Could you help me with _____ ?

> Sure.

1

2

> Could you help me with _____ ?

> Sure.

> Could you help me with _____ ?

> Sorry, I can't right now. I have to study.

3

4

TALK ABOUT POSSESSION • *WHOSE* • REVIEW: POSSESSIVE PRONOUNS AND POSSESSIVE ADJECTIVES

2
- ▶ Listen to the conversations.
- ▶ Act out similar conversations with a partner.

A Whose briefcase is this?
B It's mine. Thank you.
A You're welcome.

A Whose glasses are these?
B They're mine. Thanks.
A No problem.

3
- ▶ Study the frames.

		Possessive adjectives			Possessive pronouns		Possessive of names
Whose briefcase is this?	It's	my your his	briefcase.	It's	mine. yours. his.		It's **Rosa's** briefcase. It's **Rosa's**.
Whose keys are these?	They're	her our their	keys.	They're	hers. ours. theirs.		They're **Jack's** keys. They're **Jack's**.

4
- ▶ Work in groups. Each student puts something on a desk. Another student asks who it belongs to. Answer in as many ways as you can.

34. Let's really celebrate.

Eva and Steve's mother, Emma, is a doctor. Their father died five years ago. Emma is just getting home from work. Steve has an apartment nearby and has stopped in to say hello to his mother and sister.

1

Emma	Hi, Eva.
Eva	Hi, Mom.
Steve	Hi, Mom.
Emma	Oh, hi, Steve. How was your day?
Steve	Pretty good. Guess what?
Emma	What?
Steve	I'm running an ad for the shop on the radio.
Emma	Really? Hey, that's exciting.
Steve	Yeah. An ad agency is making it. It's going to be ready in a few days.
Emma	Well, we should celebrate. Are you going to stay for dinner?
Steve	Sure, if it's not too much trouble.
Emma	Oh, no, I'm just going to put a roast in the oven.
Steve	Do you need some help?
Emma	Sure. You can make a salad.
Eva	I'll set the table.

Eva	Just think, Mom, when I'm older and move away, you'll be able to go to a restaurant every night.
Emma	Oh, that would be too expensive. Anyway, it's no fun to go to a restaurant alone.
Eva	Maybe you'll meet somebody. You can't think about Dad forever.
Steve	Eva's right, Mom. It's not good to live in the past.
Emma	Well, as a matter of fact, I did meet someone the other day. He's an airline pilot, and he just moved into the building.
Eva	Oh, yeah? What's his name?
Emma	Tom Anderson.
Steve	Well, then, let's really celebrate. Let's all go out to dinner, and I'll treat. You can cook your roast tomorrow night.

2. Figure it out

Say *True, False,* or *It doesn't say.*

1. Steve's having dinner at his apartment.
2. Emma cooks every night.
3. Steve's ad will be on the radio soon.
4. Emma doesn't like to go out to dinner alone.
5. Steve and Eva would like their mother to meet someone nice.
6. Steve's going to take his mother and sister out for dinner.

📼 3. How to say it

Practice the conversation.

A Would you like soup or a salad?

B Soup, please.

A And would you like french fries or a baked potato?

B A baked potato.

MENU

Soup of the day
Clam chowder   Cup   Bowl
                             $2.00 $3.00

Entrees

Broiled shrimp
Fried filet of fish
Lobster
                                      $12.85
                                      $10.50
All meals include cole slaw or tossed $18.95
salad, baked potato or french fries,
and hot garlic bread.

Beverages

Coffee or tea
Soda
Iced tea
                                      $ .85
                                      $ 1.00
                                      $ 1.00

Desserts

Apple pie
Chocolate cake
Ice cream
                                      $ 2.50
                                      $ 2.00
                                      $ 2.00

4. Your turn

Emma, Eva, and Steve are having dinner at a seafood restaurant. Act out the conversations, taking the parts of Emma, Eva, Steve, and the waiter.

1. Tell the waiter you need a few more minutes. Look at the menu and decide what to order.

2. Order dinner from the menu.

3. The waiter forgot to bring water, forks, and bread, and Emma's knife is dirty. Ask the waiter for the things you need.

4. The waiter asks if you want to order dessert. Ask the waiter what desserts they have. Then order dessert. Steve asks for the check.

📼 5. Listen in

Another family is having dinner at the same restaurant. Read the statements below. Then listen to the conversation and say *True* or *False*.

1. The two women cleaned up the broken glass.
2. The waiter helped them right away.
3. Joey broke two glasses.

35.

Food Facts

Many people think the sandwich came from England in the eighteenth century. Others say sandwiches are an American invention. The truth is that this type of food has been with us for thousands of years. It is only its name that is not very old.

A British nobleman named John Montagu, the Earl of Sandwich (1718–1792), loved to play cards and didn't like to stop his game for meals. When he was hungry, he asked his servant to bring him a piece of meat between two slices of bread; this way he didn't have to use a fork and knife, and his hands stayed clean. He gave the sandwich its name, and this way of eating soon became popular in Europe.

Long before then, however, the ancient Romans enjoyed eating meat between two slices of bread. For centuries, people in the Middle East have stuffed barbecued lamb

and other tasty things into pita, a type of flat bread with a pocket. A long time before the Spaniards arrived in the New World in the sixteenth century, Mexicans had their own version of the sandwich: thin, round tortillas filled with beans, eggs, and cheese, and then rolled up.

What country do you think of when you hear the words *hot dog* and *hamburger*? The United States? These kinds of sandwiches are very popular in the U.S., but they were not born there.

Historians disagree on the origins of the hamburger. One story is that in the nineteenth century many Europeans immigrated to America on the German ship *Hamburg-Amerika*, which served a famous kind of Hamburg beef. The beef was hard, so it was usually chopped up before it was cooked. Nobody knows how the "Hamburg" steak got

between two pieces of bread, but the hamburger has been part of the American diet since the beginning of the twentieth century.

The hot dog also came from Germany. During the Middle Ages, European sausage makers developed local recipes and named their sausages after their cities. In 1852, the butchers of Frankfurt created the frankfurter, also called the dachshund sausage because it looked like the pet dog of one of the butchers. When the frankfurter traveled to America, both its names went with it. Vendors sold it at baseball games, shouting "Get your red-hot dachshund sausage!" A cartoonist named Tad Dorgan drew one for his newspaper in 1906. He couldn't spell the word *dachshund*, so he wrote *hot dog* instead. This name quickly replaced the others.

The Earl of Sandwich 1718–1792

Read the article. Then answer this question.

How did the sandwich, the hamburger, and the hot dog get their names?

FUNCTIONS/THEMES	LANGUAGE	FORMS
Buy stamps	How much is a letter to Taiwan? Fifty cents.	
Mail a package	How much is this package to San Juan? Let's see. That's $4.60.	
Say what you need	We need a few mushrooms.	
Talk about quantity	There are a few tomatoes. We need a little rice. There's a lot of milk.	*A few, a little,* and *a lot of* with count and mass nouns
Talk about quantity and measures	How much coffee should I get? Oh, a pound. How many eggs should I get? A dozen.	*How much* vs. *How many*
Plan a meal	Let's have steak for dinner. What do we need besides steak? Things for a salad.	
Say what a store is out of	There are no tomatoes, and they have no lettuce.	*No* vs. *not any*

Preview the conversations.

This man wrote a postcard to his family in Italy. How do you keep in touch with your friends and relatives? Do you usually write cards and letters, or do you call them by phone?

In the U.S., men are starting to do more of the housework, shopping, and cooking—especially if both the husband and wife work. Who usually does the housework and cooking in your family? Who does the shopping and other errands?

36. Doing chores

 It's Saturday, and Becky and Gino are doing some chores. Becky just finished writing checks to pay the monthly bills, and Gino is cleaning.

A

Becky Would you like some help with that?

Gino That's O.K. I can manage. Did you finish paying the bills?

Becky Yes. By the way, we have to call Jane and Andrew and tell them if we're coming to dinner.

Gino You know, I don't really feel like going anywhere tonight.

Becky Actually, I don't either.

Gino So why don't we stay home and relax? And I can make spaghetti and a salad.

Becky That's fine with me.

Gino O.K. But we have to go to the store. We don't have any spaghetti.

Becky I'll go on my way to the post office. I want to mail these bills today, and there are no stamps left.

Gino Oh, great. Could you mail this postcard for me? It's to my family.

Becky Sure.

B

Becky What do we need besides spaghetti?

Gino There's no coffee or bread . . . or butter.

Becky O.K. What else?

Gino Things for a salad. Get a head of lettuce and a few tomatoes. And there's only a little milk left.

Becky I'll get a gallon. Is that it?

Gino I think so.

Becky O.K. See you in a little while.

C

Clerk May I help you?

Becky Could I have ten 29-cent stamps, please?

Clerk Here you are. Anything else?

Becky Yes. How much is a postcard to Italy?

Clerk Forty cents.

Becky O.K. One 40-cent stamp.

Clerk Will that be all?

Becky Yes.

Clerk Let's see. That'll be $3.30.

Figure it out

1. Listen to the conversations and choose the correct answer.

1. a. Gino and Becky are relaxing today.
   b. Gino and Becky are doing chores and running errands today.

2. a. Becky and Gino want to have dinner with Jane and Andrew tonight.
   b. Becky and Gino don't feel like going anywhere tonight.

3. a. Becky bought ten 40-cent stamps at the post office.
   b. Becky bought ten 29-cent stamps at the post office.

2. Listen again and match.

1. Would you like some help with that?
2. I don't really feel like going anywhere tonight.
3. I can make spaghetti and a salad.
4. What else?
5. There's only a little milk left.
6. How much is a postcard to Italy?

a. Get a few tomatoes.
b. That's fine with me.
c. Forty cents.
d. That's O.K. I can manage.
e. Actually, I don't either.
f. I'll get a gallon.

37. How much is a postcard to Italy?

BUY STAMPS • MAIL A PACKAGE

1 ► Imagine you are in the United States and are mailing these cards and letters. Look at the postal chart and match the stamps with the cards and letters.
► Check your work with a partner.

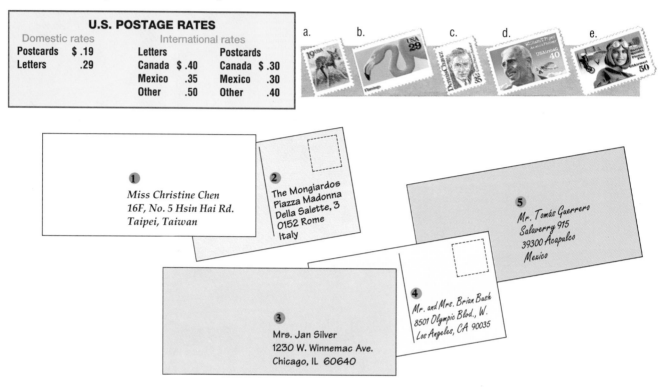

U.S. POSTAGE RATES			
Domestic rates		International rates	
Postcards $ .19		Letters	Postcards
Letters .29		Canada $ .40	Canada $ .30
		Mexico .35	Mexico .30
		Other .50	Other .40

1
Miss Christine Chen
16F, No. 5 Hsin Hai Rd.
Taipei, Taiwan

2
The Mongiardos
Piazza Madonna
Della Salette, 3
0152 Rome
Italy

5
Mr. Tomás Guerrero
Salaverry 915
39300 Acapulco
Mexico

4
Mr. and Mrs. Brian Bush
8501 Olympic Blvd., W.
Los Angeles, CA 90035

3
Mrs. Jan Silver
1230 W. Winnemac Ave.
Chicago, IL 60640

2 ► Listen to the conversation.
► Act out a similar conversation with a partner, using the other letters and cards in exercise 1.
► Work with a partner. Imagine you are at the post office where you live and need a stamp for a letter or postcard.

A How much is a letter to Taiwan?
B Fifty cents.
A O.K. One 50-cent stamp, please.

3 ► Listen to the conversation. Which package are the people talking about? Choose a, b, c, or d.
► Imagine you are mailing one of the other packages. Act out a similar conversation with a partner.

A How much is this package to San Juan?
B Let's see. That's $4.60.
A O.K.

$14.80
Mr. Joseph Goh
Pending Road, 10–32
Singapore 2367

$3.75
Ms. Lynn Babbage
870 Market St.
San Francisco, CA 94102

$9.35
Mr. and Mrs. Jaime Rúa
Camino El Otonal 2965
Santiago, Chile

Mr. Andy Aponte
Washington St., #5B
San Juan,

4 ► Listen to the rest of the conversation in exercise 3. Complete the address on the package.

38. There's only a little spaghetti left.

1 ▸ Listen and write Carlos's shopping list.
▸ Check your work with a partner.

Shopping List:
spaghetti

2 ▸ Work in groups. Say what you see in the kitchen above, using *a few*, *a little*, and *a lot of*.

A *There are a few tomatoes.*
B *There are a lot of onions.*
A *There's only a little rice.*

3 ▸ Study the frame: *A few, a little,* and *a lot of*

	a few	tomatoes. pens.	*a few* + count nouns
We need	**a little**	spaghetti. help.	*a little* + mass nouns
	a lot of	eggs. time.	*a lot of* + count or mass nouns

You can say:

a little butter or ***a few pieces of*** butter
a little bread or ***a few slices of*** bread
a little salt or ***a few spoons of*** salt

4 ▸ Complete the note with *a few* or *a little*.
▸ Check your work with a partner.

5 ▸ Imagine you are going to make dinner for a friend and you are going to stop at the store on your way home from school. Write a note to your friend saying what you are going to buy.
▸ Exchange notes with a partner to check your work.

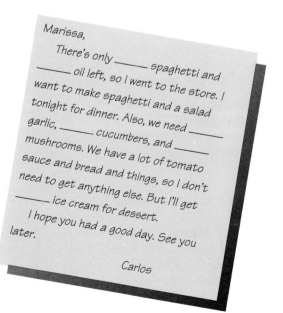

Marissa,
  There's only _____ spaghetti and
_____ oil left, so I went to the store. I
want to make spaghetti and a salad
tonight for dinner. Also, we need _____
garlic, _____ cucumbers, and _____
mushrooms. We have a lot of tomato
sauce and bread and things, so I don't
need to get anything else. But I'll get
_____ ice cream for dessert.
  I hope you had a good day. See you
later.

        Carlos

39. Do we need anything?

1 ► Check the newspaper ad below as you listen to a radio ad for the same store. There are three mistakes in the newspaper ad. What are they?

► Ask and answer questions like the ones below.

1. How much money will you save if you shop at Shopway?
2. How many locations does Shopway have?
3. How many lemons are there in a bag?
4. How much orange juice can you get for $1.79?
5. How many eggs can you get for 99¢?
6. How many ounces are there in a bottle of Brandex shampoo?

SHOPWAY
The Budget Grocery Store

SHOP NOW AND SAVE UP TO 50% on the following items

Whole Chickens **69¢/lb.**	Large California Lemons **$2.99/bag** (6/bag)
Fresh Young Lamb Chops **$2.49/lb.**	Sunshine Orange Juice **$1.79/qt.**
Elwood Homogenized Vitamin D Milk **$2.29/gal.**	Imported Swiss Cheese **$2.89/lb.**
Shopway Coffee **$3.19/lb. can**	Iceberg Lettuce **99¢/head**
Farmer's Grade A Eggs **99¢/dozen**	Home Grown Tomatoes **79¢/lb.**

Brandex Shampoo **$1.89** (16-oz. bottle)

Round-up Paper Towels **59¢/roll**

Pledge Detergent **$3.49/2-lb. box**

Prices effective through Dec. 31 at the following stores: 301 Prescott Avenue and 223 McLean Blvd.

Some specific measures and weights

1 pound (lb.) = 16 ounces (oz.)
1 pint (pt.) = 16 fluid ounces
1 quart (qt.) = 2 pints
1 gallon (gal.) = 4 quarts

1 pound = 0.45 kilo
1 quart = 0.946 liter

Some general measures

a can	a bag
a box	a bottle
a roll	a package
a loaf	a head

2 ► Study the frame: *How much* vs. *How many*

How much	coffee milk	should I get? do we need?	*How much* + mass nouns
How many	eggs lemons		*How many* + count nouns

3 ► Listen to the conversation.
► Act out the conversation with a partner, using the other items on the shopping list.

A I'm going out now. Do we need anything?
B Yes. Some coffee.
A How much should I get?
B Oh, a pound.

4 ► Imagine you are doing errands and you offered to go to the grocery store for a friend. Find out what your friend needs and make a list. Your friend will choose items from the ad in exercise 1. Be sure to find out how much—or how many—of each item your friend wants.

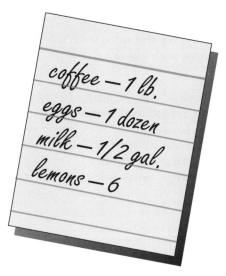

coffee — 1 lb.
eggs — 1 dozen
milk — 1/2 gal.
lemons — 6

40. There's no steak.

1 ▶ **Listen to the conversation and circle the names of the items the couple wanted to buy.**

2 ▶ **Study the frame:** *No* vs. *not any*

There	's **no** isn't **any**	steak.
They	have **no** don't have **any**	

3 ▶ **Listen to the two possible conversations.**
▶ **Practice the conversations with a partner.**
▶ **Look at the picture in exercise 1. Act out a similar conversation with a partner, saying what the store is out of.**

A Let's have steak for dinner tonight.
B There's no steak.
A How about lamb chops?

B O.K. What do we need besides lamb chops?
A Things for a salad.
B There are no tomatoes, and they have no lettuce.
A I can't believe this store.
B I can't either. Let's go somewhere else.
A That's fine with me.

B There are no lamb chops either.
A I can't believe this store.
B I can't either. Let's go somewhere else.
A That's fine with me.

4 ▶ **Interview your classmates. Find out each person's favorite meal.**

41. You forget things, too . . .

Eva is just getting home from school. Bobby is with her.

①

Eva What's all this? I mailed these bills for Mom yesterday, and the post office sent them back.

Bobby Look. You forgot to put stamps on them.

Eva Oh, how stupid!

Bobby Yeah, it sure was. I can't believe it.

Eva Don't make fun of me. You forget things, too . . . like the time you left the water running in the bathtub and flooded the apartment downstairs . . . and the time . . .

Bobby O.K., O.K.

Eva Anyway, I'm worried about these bills. They're going to be late unless I mail them right away.

Bobby Got any stamps?

Eva I don't know. I don't know where Mom keeps them.

Bobby I have to go to the post office later anyway, so I can mail your letters. How many stamps do you need?

Eva Could you buy a book?

Bobby How much does a book cost?

Eva I think there are 20 stamps in a book, so I guess $5.80. Here's some money. I'm sure that's enough.

Bobby O.K. See you later.

Eva Bobby, wait. You forgot to take the bills.

Bobby No, I didn't. You forgot to give them to me.

2. Figure it out

Say *True, False,* or *It doesn't say.*

1. Eva mailed her mother's bills last week.
2. Bobby made fun of Eva.
3. Eva doesn't want the bills to be late.
4. Bobby is going to buy a book of stamps for Eva.
5. Bobby will mail the bills before he goes to the post office.
6. Bobby will forget to put stamps on the envelopes before he mails them.

At the post office, Bobby sees a woman who is having difficulty carrying a package. Read the statements below. Then listen to the conversation and choose *a* or *b*.

1. At first, the woman thinks she _____ manage.
   a. can
   b. can't

2. Later, the woman _____ help from Bobby.
   a. accepts
   b. refuses

3. Bobby _____ the package is heavy.
   a. thinks
   b. doesn't think

4. The package weighs _____ pounds.
   a. forty
   b. forty-five

▭ **4. How to say it**

Practice the conversation.

A Could you get some stamps?

B Sure. Anything else?

A Yes. Some coffee, bread, and milk.

B O.K.

A And some eggs, butter, and a little cheese.

5. Your turn

The customer above is buying some stamps. She wants to send eight letters and five postcards to Hawaii. Act out the conversation between the customer and the clerk.

42.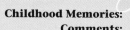

A TASTE FOR CHARITY

Name: Paul Newman
Place of Birth: Cleveland, Ohio
Most Famous Films: *Cool Hand Luke* (1967)
Butch Cassidy and the Sundance Kid (1969)
The Sting (1973)
The Color of Money (1986; won the Academy Award for Best Actor, 1987)
Interests: Cooking, writing poetry, and painting
Dislikes: When people think of him more for his blue eyes and good looks than for his talent
When he has to talk about himself and answer the same questions over and over
Childhood Memories: Summer camp—the simple life, being close to nature and friends
Comments: "I've admired and appreciated the guy since I was twelve years old and in a movie theater." (Martin Scorsese, director)
"He's got a great sense of humor." (Tom Cruise, co-star of *The Color of Money*)
"I. . . think that in life we need to be a little like the farmer who puts back into the soil what he takes out." (Newman)

Paul Newman has had a long career as a famous movie star—he's played a leading man for 30 years, acted in over 45 films, and won an Oscar for Best Actor in 1987. He has been married to the actress Joanne Woodward since 1958 and has appeared together with her in films as well as directed her.

But there are many sides to Newman. He enjoys having a little risk in his life and is known for being a champion race-car driver. He has always liked to cook, and when friends loved his Christmas presents of homemade salad dressing, Newman decided to go into business. Begun in 1982, Newman's Own took off and became a success. Soon spaghetti sauce, popcorn, and lemonade were added, all carrying the familiar drawing of Newman's smiling face on their labels. Even Burger King restaurants serve the salad dressings.

Paul Newman believes in helping other people. All the profits from his successful food business are donated to charity. A charity close to his heart is The-Hole-in-the-Wall-Gang Camp for children with cancer and other serious diseases, which he began in 1988. This is a place where children can get away from the hospital atmosphere for two weeks and pretend they are living in the Wild West during the time of the American cowboy.

1. **Read the article. Then scan it and find the words for:**

   a. four occupations.
   b. four things to eat or drink.
   c. a holiday.

2. **Look at the article again and find this information:**

   a. the things Paul Newman likes to do in his free time.
   b. the year Paul Newman won an Academy Award.
   c. Newman's wife's name and occupation.
   d. the name of Paul Newman's camp for sick children.

3. **Are there any important charities in your country?**
   Do people in your country give money and time to charities?

Review of units 5–7

1A ▸ Student A follows the instructions below.
Student B follows the instructions on page 78.

Student A   Read the newspaper articles below. First, invite your partner to go to the fair and answer any questions your partner has. Second, accept your partner's invitation to the film festival. Ask your partner questions about the film festival to fill in the blanks in the newspaper article.

This Week

Enjoy Family Fun at the Agricultural Fair

It's that time again. The Agricultural Fair opens today, October 8, and runs to October 22—two weeks of fun for the whole family. So, put on your most comfortable shoes and come to the County Fairgrounds at Washington Avenue and State Road 41. Exhibits and rides will be open from 10 a.m. until 11 p.m. every day.

This year the fair offers a variety of animals, rides, and exhibits, so get ready to enjoy the Ferris wheel, eat cotton candy, and pet all the smelly but lovable animals.

One of the most unbelievable exhibits is called "Too big to eat." Here you can see huge cucumbers, cabbages, and other vegetables, some weighing up to 15 pounds.

There are plenty of places to eat at the fair. You'll find a great variety of international food as well as favorite snacks such as french fries, cotton candy, candy apples, and popcorn.

Admission to the fair is $6.50 for adults and $3.50 for children under 12.

French Film Festival

The fourth annual French Film Festival starts _____ . From Friday to Sunday they are playing _____ — everything from family comedies to romantic dramas. Admission to each film is $5. You can buy tickets in advance at _____ at 44533 Wilton Boulevard or by calling 555-9753. But act quickly because some shows are already sold out. For more information about each film, _____ at the theater.

Schedule of Films

Friday
5:00 p.m.—*L'Homme de Ma Vie* ("The Man of My Life")
7:30 p.m.—*Après L'Amour* ("After Love")
10:00 p.m.—*Tito et Moi* ("Tito and Me")

Saturday
10:00 a.m.—*L'Homme de Ma Vie* ("The Man of My Life")
1:00 p.m.—*Indochine* ("Indochina")
3:30 p.m.—*Après L'Amour* ("After Love")
5:00 p.m.—*Tito et Moi* ("Tito and Me")
7:30 p.m.— _____
10:00 p.m.—*Max et Jeremie* ("Max and Jeremy")

Sunday
1:00 p.m.—*Indochine* ("Indochina")
3:30 p.m.—*Le Petit Prince A Dit* ("The Little Prince Said")
5:00 p.m.—*Tito et Moi* ("Tito and Me")
7:30 p.m.—*Novembre* ("November")
10:00 p.m.—*Les Nuits Fauves* ("Wild Nights")

2 ▸ George and Ellen are at the fair with their two-year-old son, Mike. They are reading the rules for the Ferris wheel. Work with a partner and complete the rules with the imperatives in the box.

Enjoy/Don't enjoy
Have/Don't have
Bring/Don't bring
Wait/Don't wait
Stand up/Don't stand up
Take/Don't take

Don't bring children under five on the Ferris wheel.
_____ in line until it's your turn to get on.
_____ your ticket ready.
_____ during the ride.
_____ food or drinks on the ride.
_____ your ride.

3 ▸ Work with a partner and answer the question: Can George and Ellen take their son on the Ferris wheel?

1B ▶ Student B follows the instructions below.
Student A follows the instructions on page 77.

Student A follows the instructions on page 77.

Student B Read the newspaper articles below. First, accept your partner's invitation to the fair. Ask your partner questions about the fair to fill in the blanks in the newspaper article. Second, invite your partner to the film festival and answer any questions your partner has.

This Week

Enjoy Family Fun at the Agricultural Fair

It's that time again. The Agricultural Fair opens _____ and runs to October 22—two weeks of fun for the whole family. So, put on your most comfortable shoes and come to the County Fairgrounds at _____. Exhibits and rides will be open from _____ every day.

This year the fair offers _____, so get ready to enjoy the Ferris wheel, eat cotton candy, and pet all the smelly but lovable animals.

One of the most unbelievable exhibits is called "Too big to eat." Here you can see huge cucumbers, cabbages, and other vegetables, some weighing up to 15 pounds.

There are plenty of places to eat at the fair. You'll find a great variety of international food as well as favorite snacks such as french fries, cotton candy, candy apples, and popcorn.

Admission to the fair is _____.

French Film Festival

The fourth annual French Film Festival starts tomorrow, Friday, October 9. From Friday to Sunday they are playing eight different films—everything from family comedies to romantic dramas. Admission to each film is $5. You can buy tickets in advance at the Coleman Art Theater at 44533 Wilton Boulevard or by calling 555-9753. But act quickly because some shows are already sold out. For more information about each film, you can get a brochure at the theater.

Schedule of Films

Friday
5:00 p.m.—*L'Homme de Ma Vie* ("The Man of My Life")
7:30 p.m.—*Après L'Amour* ("After Love")
10:00 p.m.—*Tito et Moi* ("Tito and Me")

Saturday
10:00 a.m.—*L'Homme de Ma Vie* ("The Man of My Life")
1:00 p.m.—*Indochine* ("Indochina")
3:30 p.m.—*Après L'Amour* ("After Love")
5:00 p.m.—*Tito et Moi* ("Tito and Me")
7:30 p.m.—*Novembre* ("November")
10:00 p.m.—*Max et Jeremie* ("Max and Jeremy")

Sunday
1:00 p.m.—*Indochine* ("Indochina")
3:30 p.m.—*Le Petit Prince A Dit* ("The Little Prince Said")
5:00 p.m.—*Tito et Moi* ("Tito and Me")
7:30 p.m.—*Novembre* ("November")
10:00 p.m.—*Les Nuits Fauves* ("Wild Nights")

4 ▶ George and Ellen are hungry. Complete George's part of the conversation below.

Ellen Well, we can't go on the Ferris wheel, so let's get something to eat.
George _____
Ellen How about that tent over there?
George _____
Ellen Could you help me with the baby?
George _____
Ellen You take the baby, and I'll take the stroller and the toys.

5 ▶ Listen to the conversation and list the things Ellen orders.
▶ Work in groups of three. One of you will be the waiter or waitress, the other two will be customers. Imagine you are at the fair and order something to eat. Also ask for *another napkin, some water,* and *the check.*

6 ▶ **Complete Ellen's part of the conversation.**

George I forgot to tell you. I'm going to Taiwan on business.

Ellen _____

George In the spring. In April.

Ellen _____

George It's usually very warm and humid.

Ellen _____

George I'm probably going to stay for two weeks.

Ellen _____

George An airline ticket to Taiwan? Oh, about $1,000.00.

7 ▶ **The cook is talking to himself. Complete his sentences with *a*, *some*, and *any*.**

We need _____ plastic forks. And we don't have _____ plastic spoons, so we need _____ of those. Let's see, oh, _____ big bottle of oil, _____ mustard, _____ ketchup, and _____ paper napkins. And we need _____ box of dish detergent. There isn't _____ left.

8 ▶ **Complete the conversation.**

Waiter _____

Waitress I think it's hers—the woman with the baby.

9 ▶ **Play a game.**

Work in groups. Put several of your group's possessions in a bag. Exchange bags with another group. Try to find the owner of each item in your new bag, acting out the conversation in exercise 8.

10 ▶ Complete the conversation with *a lot (of)*, *a little*, *a few*, and *no*.

Ellen I have to stop at the grocery store for _____ minutes on the way home and then go to the post office. Do you want to come along?

George Why don't you go to the post office and I'll go to the store? It'll be faster.

Ellen O.K. Good idea.

George So, what do we need from the store?

Ellen Well, there's only _____ milk—maybe enough for one cup of coffee—and we have _____ bread. We finished it for breakfast.

George O.K. A gallon of milk and a loaf of bread. Are we going to get something for dinner?

Ellen Yeah. I thought we'd get _____ lamb chops. We have _____ potatoes, a whole bag, I think, so we can have lamb chops and mashed potatoes.

George Oh, you know, there are _____ tomatoes. There were a couple in the refrigerator, but they were rotten so I threw them out.

Ellen How many should we get?

George Oh, _____, two or three. And _____ lettuce. We don't need _____

Ellen Anything else?

George Yeah. There's _____ butter. We need a pound.

11 ▶ Ask and answer questions about the conversation in exercise 10, using *how much* and *how many*.

How much milk are they going to buy?
How many lamb chops are they going to get?

12 ▶ Work in a group and plan a meal at one of your houses. Make a list of things you will need. Tell the group what you can bring from home and write your name after the item(s) on the list. Then check (√) the things the group will have to buy at the store.

13 ▶ Work with a partner. Imagine that one of you is a post office clerk and that the other needs a stamp to send a postcard to another country. Act out the conversation.

FUNCTIONS/THEMES	LANGUAGE	FORMS
Talk about moods and feelings	You're in a good mood today! Yeah. I just got some good news. You look upset. Is anything wrong? I'm just in a bad mood. I always get nervous when I have to take a test.	*Just* for the recent past Clauses with *when, as soon as, before,* and *after*
Suggest a possible activity Accept or reject a suggestion	Why don't we do something? Maybe we could go to a movie. That's a good idea. No. I don't feel like going anywhere. I'm not in the mood.	*Could* Indefinite compounds: *something, anything, nothing,* etc.
Ask for and give opinions	What did you think of the movie? I liked it a lot. I didn't enjoy it at all.	Review: the simple past tense
Talk about plans	What are you doing tonight? I'm having a party.	The present continuous as future

Preview the conversations.

Many things can put you in a good mood—for example, passing a test, meeting a good friend, or seeing a wonderful movie. What puts you in a good mood?

Some things that put people in a bad mood are failing a test, feeling sick, and not having enough money. What puts you in a bad mood or makes you feel depressed?

43. Moods and feelings

Janet and Gary are close friends. They talk about why they feel good or feel depressed.

A

Janet You look upset. Is anything wrong?

Gary Oh, I'm just in a bad mood today.

Janet Why?

Gary I think I failed my math test.

Janet Oh, you probably passed.

Gary Well, maybe, but I always get nervous when I have to take a test.

Janet A lot of people do. But don't worry about it. You always do well in math.

B

Janet You're in a good mood today!

Gary Yeah. I just got some good news. We got our math tests back this morning.

Janet And?

Gary I didn't fail after all. In fact, I only made one mistake.

Janet That's great!

Gary Yeah. Hey, you look pretty happy today, too.

Janet I am! Exams are over and I'm having a party tonight. I hope you're still going to come.

Gary Of course. It sounds like fun. Can I bring anything?

Janet No, nothing. Everyone's coming around 8:00.

Gary O.K. See you then.

C

Gary You look tired.

Janet Oh, I just feel a little depressed. I always feel that way on Sunday afternoons.

Gary Really? Why?

Janet Because the weekend's almost over.

Gary Well, why don't we do something? Maybe we could go to a movie.

Janet No. I don't feel like going anywhere. I'm not in the mood.

Gary Come on, you need to get out of here. Me too. *Lucky in Love* is playing at the Baronet. Why don't we go see it?

Janet It is? Well, . . . O.K. Maybe you're right.

D

Janet What did you think of the movie?

Gary I didn't like it at all.

Janet Really? Why not?

Gary I don't know. I just didn't think it was very funny. How did you like it?

Janet I liked it a lot. It really put me in a good mood.

Figure it out

1. Listen and choose *a* or *b* to complete the sentences.

1. At first Gary thinks he failed his math test, so
   a. he is in a good mood.
   b. he is in a bad mood.

2. The next day Gary is in a good mood because
   a. he passed his math test.
   b. he's going to Janet's party.

3. On Sunday Janet is in a bad mood because
   a. the weekend is almost over.
   b. she hates to study.

4. Later Janet is in a good mood because
   a. she enjoyed the movie.
   b. the weekend is almost over.

2. Listen again and match.

1. You look upset. What's wrong?
2. I always get nervous when I have to take a test.
3. You're in a good mood!
4. Can I bring anything?
5. Why don't we do something?
6. You need to get out of here.
7. What did you think of the movie?
8. Why not?

a. No, I don't feel like going anywhere.
b. Maybe you're right.
c. Yeah. I just got some good news.
d. I didn't like it at all.
e. No, nothing.
f. I just didn't think it was very funny.
g. A lot of people do.
h. Oh, I'm just in a bad mood.

44. You look upset.

1 ▸ The people in the pictures are in a bad mood. Make a comment to complete each exchange. Use the words in the box. In some of the exchanges, there is more than one possible comment.

▸ Listen to the possible exchanges.

| a. depressed | c. scared | e. tired |
| b. nervous | d. angry | f. bored |

You look _____.
I just got some bad news. [1]

You look _____.
I know. I stayed up late last night. [2]

You look _____.
I am. I don't have anything to do. [3]

You look _____.
I always get nervous when I fly. [4]

You look _____.
I always get scared when I'm home alone. [5]

You look _____.
I am! I had a two o'clock appointment, but my doctor didn't see me until four thirty! [6]

2 ▸ Listen to the conversation.
▸ Imagine you are one of the people in exercise 1. Practice similar conversations with a partner.

A You look upset. Is anything wrong?
B Oh, I'm just in a bad mood.
A Why?
B I think I failed my math test.
A Oh, you probably passed.
B Well, maybe. I always get nervous when I have to take a test.
A A lot of people do.

I always get . . .

nervous	before I take a trip.
scared	when I fly.
angry	when someone is late.
depressed	after I read the newspaper.
upset	when I fail a test.

3 ▸ Listen to the conversation.
▸ Imagine something put you in a good mood. Have a similar conversation with a partner.

A You're in a good mood today!
B Yeah. I just got some good news. I passed my math test.
A That's great!

Some things that put people in a good mood

I passed my exam.
I just got a check from my father.
I just moved into my new apartment.
I started my new job today.
I'm having a party tonight.

With the past tense, *just* often means "very recently."	With all tenses, *just* can also mean "only."
I **just** got some good news.	I **just** had toast for breakfast. Nothing else.
I **just** moved into my new apartment.	I **just** have two dollars.
I was **just** there.	I'm **just** going to study English tonight.

4 ▶ **Study the frame.**

Clauses with *when, as soon as, before,* and *after*		
I always get upset	**when**	I fail a test.
They have dinner	**as soon as**	they get home.
She studies hard	**before**	she takes a test.
He goes to class	**after**	he finishes work.

You can also say:

When I fail a test, I always get upset.
As soon as they get home, they have dinner.
Before she takes a test, she studies hard.
After he finishes work, he goes to class.

Notice the comma in these sentences.

5 ▶ **A woman wrote a letter to a radio show called "Tell Us Your Problem." Complete this paragraph from her letter with *when, before, after,* and *as soon as.* There may be more than one possibility for some items.**

I'm always in a bad mood _____ business trip. It's not too bad _____ I'm getting ready for a train. However, I get nervous _____ I drive or take a _____ I get on a plane, I hold the arms of my seat so tight that my hands turn white. _____ the flight attendant offers something to drink or eat, I refuse. I'm afraid I'll get sick. And I can't even talk _____ someone tries to strike up a conversation. _____ the plane lands, I feel much better. And I'm usually very hungry. So, _____ I get off, I go to the airport cafeteria. Finally, I get something to eat and relax!

6 ▶ **Now listen to the advice from the host of "Tell Us Your Problem." Then choose *a* or *b* to complete each statement.**

1. The host of "Tell Us Your Problem" agrees that
   a. a lot of people don't like to fly.
   b. most people like to fly.

2. The host suggests that passengers think about
   a. the positive things about flying.
   b. the negative things about flying.

3. The host says
   a. there are more automobile accidents than airplane accidents.
   b. there are more airplane accidents than automobile accidents.

4. He suggests
   a. holding your seat tight and not eating.
   b. reading a good book or taking a nap.

5. If absolutely necessary, he suggests
   a. staying home.
   b. getting a prescription from a doctor.

7 ▶ **Talk with your classmates. Tell them what puts you in a good or bad mood. Your classmates will offer advice.**

45. Why don't we do something?

1 ▶ **Listen to the two possible conversations.**
▶ **Have a similar conversation with a partner.**

A You look tired.
B Oh, I just feel a little depressed. I always feel
that way on Sunday afternoons.
A Really? Why?
B Because the weekend's almost over.
A Well, why don't we do something? Maybe we could go to a movie.

B That's a good idea.   **B** No. I don't feel like going anywhere. I'm not in the mood.

> **Some possible activities**
>
> Maybe we could . . .
> go to a movie.
> go out for dinner.
> go for a walk.
> go for a drive.

2 ▶ **Study the frames: Indefinite compounds**

Affirmative statements	Negative statements
Let's do **something**.	I don't feel like doing **anything**.
Let's go **somewhere**.	I don't feel like going **anywhere**.
Let's invite **someone** over.	I don't feel like seeing **anyone**.

someone = somebody
anyone = anybody
no one = nobody

I don't feel like seeing anybody.

Yes-no questions	Negative short answers
Do you want to do **anything**?	No, **nothing**.
Do you want to go **anywhere**?	No, **nowhere**.
Do you want to invite **anyone** over?	No, **no one**.

You can also use *something, somewhere,*
and *someone* in questions.

Do you want to do something?

3 ▶ **Complete the movie reviews with appropriate
indefinite compounds.**

A Summer Holiday

Elliot doesn't feel like seeing _____ after his
wife leaves him. He just wants to go _____
and be alone. But in Hawaii he meets Sarah,
_____ new and exciting. He doesn't know
_____ about Sarah, but he thinks she's
hiding _____ from her past. Two strangers
find romance in this mysterious love story.

SPACE MONSTERS

Strange monsters from
_____ in the galaxy
invade the planet Xenon.
King Astro can think of
_____ or nothing to stop
them. Queen Larena might
know _____ that can
help, but she's afraid to tell
_____ about their
problem. Can the scientist Dr.
Strom help them before
_____ terrible happens?
This science fiction adventure
is out of this world!

4 ▶ **Listen to the movie review. Check (√) the things the film critic liked about the movie.**
▶ **Which movie did the critic see, *A Summer Holiday* or *Space Monsters*?**

_____ the acting   _____ the costumes   _____ the makeup
_____ the story   _____ the special effects   _____ the music

5 ▶ **Listen to the two possible conversations.**
▶ **Have a similar conversation with a partner.**

A What did you think of the movie?

B I didn't like it at all.

A Really? Why not?

B I don't know. I just didn't think it was very funny. How did you like it?

A I liked it a lot.

B I liked it a lot. The story was fascinating. How did you like it?

A I didn't enjoy it at all.

Some reasons

The story was fascinating.
It showed a whole different way of life.
The acting was excellent.
The music was wonderful.
I loved the food.
The story was terrible.
I didn't learn anything new.
It wasn't very interesting.
It lasted too long.
The service was awful.

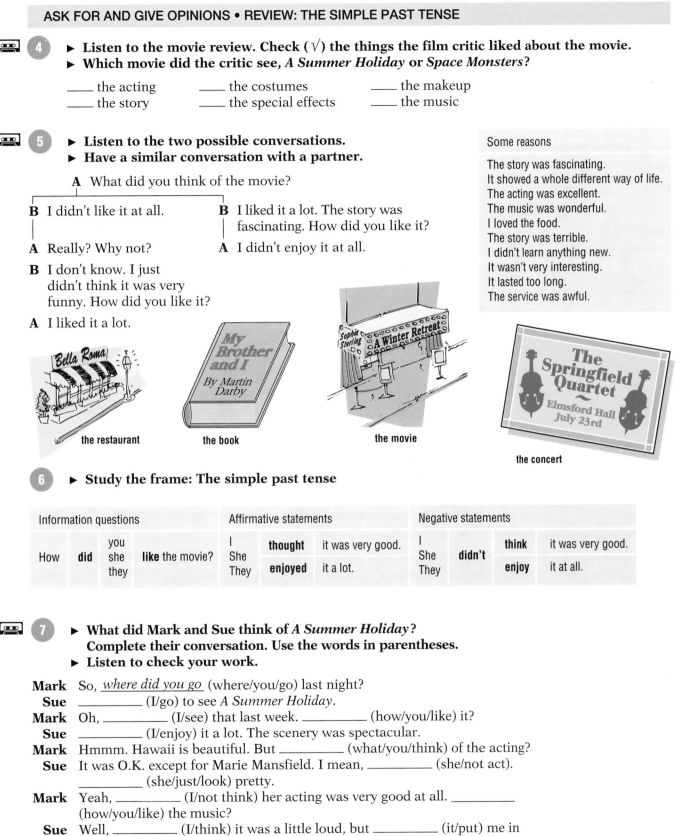

the restaurant   the book   the movie   the concert

6 ▶ **Study the frame: The simple past tense**

Information questions				Affirmative statements			Negative statements			
How	did	you she they	like the movie?	I She They	**thought**	it was very good.	I She They	**didn't**	**think**	it was very good.
					enjoyed	it a lot.			**enjoy**	it at all.

7 ▶ **What did Mark and Sue think of *A Summer Holiday*?**
Complete their conversation. Use the words in parentheses.
▶ **Listen to check your work.**

Mark So, _where did you go_ (where/you/go) last night?
Sue _____ (I/go) to see *A Summer Holiday*.
Mark Oh, _____ (I/see) that last week. _____ (how/you/like) it?
Sue _____ (I/enjoy) it a lot. The scenery was spectacular.
Mark Hmmm. Hawaii is beautiful. But _____ (what/you/think) of the acting?
Sue It was O.K. except for Marie Mansfield. I mean, _____ (she/not act).
_____ (she/just/look) pretty.
Mark Yeah, _____ (I/not think) her acting was very good at all. _____
(how/you/like) the music?
Sue Well, _____ (I/think) it was a little loud, but _____ (it/put) me in a good mood.

8 ▶ **Talk to your classmates. Tell them about a movie or TV show you saw, or a book you read recently. Tell why you liked or didn't like it.**

46. You look pretty happy today.

1 ▶ What are these people thinking? Match the thoughts in the box with the pictures.
▶ Listen to check your work.

a. I'm going on vacation tomorrow.
b. We're moving into our new apartment this weekend.
c. I'm getting married next week.
d. I'm starting a new job on Monday.
e. I'm having a party tonight.
f. I'm leaving work early today.

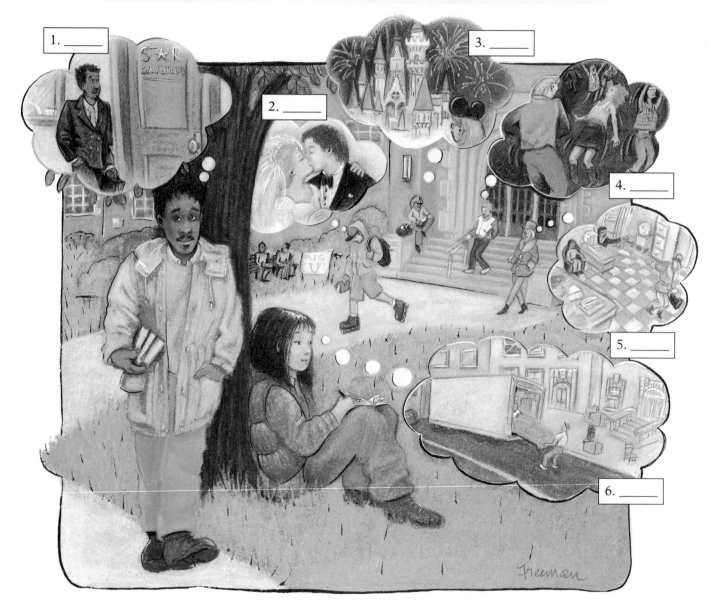

2 ▶ Listen to the conversation.
▶ Work with a partner. Practice similar conversations using the information in exercise 1 or your own good news.

A You look pretty happy today.
B I am. I'm having a party tonight.
A That sounds like fun.

Some responses

That's great!	That's really good news.
How exciting!	I'm really happy for you.
That sounds like fun.	Lucky you!

3 ▶ **Listen to the four conversations. Then match the two parts of the sentences.**

1. Melanie is
2. Sally and Tim are
3. Jack is
4. The Carvers are

a. having dinner in a Chinese restaurant.
b. moving to Hawaii.
c. getting ready for a trip.
d. coming home on Friday.

4 ▶ **Study the frame.**

Present continuous as future	You can often use the present continuous to talk about plans and intentions.
What **are** you **doing** tonight? I'**m having** a party.	*What are you doing tonight?* means *What are you going to do tonight?* *I'm having a party.* means *I'm going to have a party.*

5 ▶ **Complete the four conversations, using the present continuous as future and the verbs in parentheses.**
▶ **Listen to check your work.**

Hey, Melanie, _____ (do) tonight?

Not much. I have to get ready for my trip.

Oh, _____ (leave)?

Tomorrow.

Sally and I _____ (go) out for dinner tonight. Do you want to come?

To the Chinese restaurant across the street.

Well, maybe, Tim. _____ (go)?

1

2

Did you know? Jack _____ (move) to California.

_____ (move) to California. _____ (move) to Hawaii.

Hawaii! We'll never see him again.

I _____ (have) a party, so I called the Carvers. But they weren't home.

They're away, but _____ (come) home on Friday.

3

4

6 ▶ **Talk to your classmates.**

Make a comment to one of your classmates. Your classmate will tell you about a real or imagined future plan. Ask any appropriate questions.

A *You look happy today.*
B *I am. I'm going to a concert tonight.*
A . . .

47. What kind of car is that?

Steve's working at the shop when Russell Evans comes in.

1

Russell Hi. I'm having a problem with my car. I heard your ad on the radio and I thought maybe you could fix it.

Steve What's the matter with it?

Russell It's the engine. It's making a funny noise.

Steve Let's take a look at it. Is it parked outside?

Russell Yes. It's over there.

Steve Wow! What kind of car is that?

Russell It's a 1949 Peugeot.

Steve No kidding. Where did you get it?

Russell I bought it from a movie studio in Hollywood.

Steve Really? I've never seen one before. (*He looks under the hood.*)

Russell There aren't too many around. . . . You know, your ad says you can fix anything, but you look a little worried.

Steve Yeah . . . well . . . I'll see what I can do.

(*Thirty minutes later*)

Steve I'm sorry, sir, but I can't find the problem. I've never worked on anything like this before.

Russell But your ad says you can fix anything.

Steve I can. I mean . . . uh . . . it's such an old model. I don't think anyone could fix it.

2. Figure it out

Put the events in the correct order.

___ Steve asked Russell Evans where he got the car.
___ Steve said that he couldn't find the problem.
___ Russell Evans heard Steve's ad on the radio.
___ Russell Evans said that he bought his car from a movie studio in Hollywood.
___ Steve wrote an ad for his shop.
___ Russell Evans brought his car to Steve's shop.
___ Steve tried to fix the car.

🔲 3. Listen in

Bob and Margaret are talking about the car that Steve is trying to fix. Read the statements below. Then listen to the conversation and fill in the missing words.

1. The man looks _____ .
2. Bob gets _____ when he works on expensive cars.

🔲 4. How to say it

Practice the words. Then practice the conversation.

failed	[feyld]	[d]
passed	[pæst]	[t]
wanted	[wantəd]	[əd]

A I think I failed my business test.
B I'm sure you passed.
A I don't know. I wanted to study more, but I was so tired.

5. Your turn

Michael is worried about his business mid-term exam. He's talking to his friend Paul while Bob works on his car. Act out the conversation.

Paul You seem a little depressed. What's the matter?
Michael _____
Paul Why are you worried about it?
Michael _____
Paul I'm sure you passed.
Michael _____
Paul A lot of people get nervous.
Michael _____
Paul You need to take a break. Why don't we go to a movie?
Michael _____
Paul *The Lost Galaxy* is at the State Theater.
Michael _____
Paul Great! Let's go.

48.

DEAR MAGGIE

by Margaret Vanderhorn

DEAR MAGGIE: Sometimes I think there's really something wrong with me. I am a college student. I have a few close friends, and I go out on dates <u>occasionally</u>. The <u>trouble</u> starts when I go to a party. I always feel a little nervous before I get there. After I'm there, I get upset with myself because I can't find anything to say to people. I guess I'm just not a <u>good conversationalist</u>. I'm much better when I'm with only a few people. What should I do?
— DEPRESSED

DEAR DEPRESSED: It sounds like you're a little shy. There's nothing wrong with that. Most young people who are shy gain more <u>confidence</u> when they get a little older. In any case, try not to worry about it. If you get upset with yourself, it just makes <u>matters</u> worse. I have a suggestion which could help. Why don't you have a party and invite only your close friends and other people you know well? Small parties can be more fun than big ones. This could also be an opportunity to show how <u>outgoing</u> you really can be.

DEAR MAGGIE: My mother lives in another city, and she comes to visit us for two weeks every year. The problem is that when she comes, she always thinks she has to do everything around the house. My husband and I both work. When we come home in the evening, dinner is ready, the house is <u>absolutely</u> <u>spotless</u>, and the kids have had their baths and are in their pajamas. But my mother has worked so hard that she's nervous, <u>irritable</u>, and very unpleasant to be with for the rest of the evening. I have tried to tell her not to do so much housework, but she won't listen. Is there anything I can do?
— A WORRIED DAUGHTER

DEAR WORRIED DAUGHTER: Your mother probably feels a strong need to be useful, and to prove to you that she's a good guest. But maybe she's also trying to tell you something. It sounds like she's at home most of the day while you and your husband are at work. Maybe she just feels bored and <u>neglected</u> and would like more attention from you. Why don't you schedule her next visit when you can take some time off from work? That way you can share the responsibilities around the house and also get out of the house and do things together. This could make things better.

1. **Read the advice column. Then look at each underlined word and choose the best answer.**

1. *Occasionally* means
   a. not very often.
   b. often.

2. *Trouble* means
   a. terrible.
   b. problem.

3. A *good conversationalist* is
   a. someone who speaks well and talks a lot.
   b. someone who is quiet and doesn't talk much.

4. *Confidence* means
   a. not being sure of one's ability.
   b. belief in one's own ability.

5. *Matters* means
   a. things.
   b. upset.

6. *Outgoing* means
   a. friendly.
   b. unfriendly.

7. *Absolutely* means
   a. completely or definitely.
   b. not very.

8. *Spotless* means
   a. very dirty.
   b. very clean.

9. *Irritable* means
   a. easily made angry by small things.
   b. happy and relaxed.

10. *Neglected* means
    a. getting too much attention.
    b. not getting enough attention.

2. **Do you agree or disagree with the advice Maggie gives to each person?**

PREVIEW

FUNCTIONS/THEMES	LANGUAGE	FORMS
Find out what's wrong	What's the matter? I broke my leg.	
Make a recommendation	I'd better go call for help.	*Had better*
Call for help	My friend just fell off a ladder. Could you send an ambulance?	
Report an emergency	There's a fire at 33 Bank Street.	
Explain what happened	What happened to you? I broke my ankle. When did it happen? The day before yesterday. Did you have to go to the hospital? Yes, I did.	The simple past tense: yes-no questions Expressions of past time
Talk about past activities	Did you have a good weekend? It wasn't bad. What did you do? I went camping.	Review: the simple past tense of irregular verbs

Preview the conversations.

These two women went biking last weekend.
What did you do? Did you have a good time?

Did you ever have an accident? Did you have to get help?
Is there a special telephone number you can call in an emergency?

49. Are you O.K.?

 Anne Burgess and Cindy Wu are on a weekend bike trip.

A

Cindy Anne, watch out!
Anne Wha . . . Oh . . . Ow!
Cindy Are you O.K.?
Anne Uh, I don't think so.
Cindy What's the matter?
Anne I think I broke my ankle. It really hurts.
Cindy I'd better go call for help. Stay here.

B

Operator 911.
Cindy My friend just had a bicycle accident. I think she broke her ankle. Could you send an ambulance?
Operator Could I have your name, please?
Cindy Yes, it's Cindy Wu.
Operator And where's the emergency?
Cindy Near the rest area on Route 60.
Operator All right, Ms. Wu. Stay calm. We'll send an ambulance right away.

C

Nurse What happened?
Anne Oh, I fell off my bike and hurt my ankle. It feels like it's broken.
Nurse Do you have medical insurance, Miss Burgess?
Anne Yes. Would you like to see my insurance card?
Nurse Yes, please. . . . All right. A doctor will be with you in a minute.

D

Pablo Hi, Anne. Did you have a good weekend?

Anne It was so-so.

Pablo What did you do?

Anne Well, I went biking in Evergreen National Park with Cindy Wu, and . . .

Pablo Hey, what happened to you?

Anne That's the bad part. I ran into a rock and fell off my bike. I broke my ankle.

Pablo When did it happen?

Anne The day before yesterday—Saturday. Unfortunately, it was the first day of our trip.

Pablo Did you have to go to the hospital?

Anne Yes, I did. I couldn't walk at all.

Pablo Gee, that's terrible.

Anne Oh, I'll be O.K. in a month or two. So, how was your weekend?

Pablo Not bad. I didn't do anything special. I just stayed home and painted the house.

Figure it out

1. Listen to the conversations and choose the correct answers.

1. a. Cindy had a bicycle accident.
   b. Anne fell off her bike and broke her ankle.
2. a. Anne's ankle will be O.K. in a day or two.
   b. Anne's ankle will be O.K. in a month or two.

2. Listen again and say *True* or *False*.

1. Anne hurt her ankle.
2. Cindy called 911, the telephone number for emergencies.
3. An ambulance took Anne to the hospital.
4. Anne doesn't have medical insurance.
5. Anne's accident happened the day before yesterday.
6. Pablo went swimming last weekend.

3. Match.

1. Are you O.K.?
2. What's the matter?
3. Where's the emergency?
4. When did it happen?
5. How was your weekend?

a. The day before yesterday.
b. I think I broke my ankle.
c. Not bad.
d. Near the rest area on Route 60.
e. I don't think so.

4. Find the simple past tense form of these verbs.

1. fall
2. break
3. hurt
4. go
5. have
6. run

50. What's the matter?

FIND OUT WHAT'S WRONG • MAKE A RECOMMENDATION • CALL FOR HELP • REPORT AN EMERGENCY

1 ► What does each person say? Match the pictures with the sentences.
► Listen to check your answers.

1. _____ 2. _____ 3. _____
4. _____ 5. _____ 6. _____

a. I cut my hand on Saturday, but it wasn't serious. I put on a bandage at home.
b. I broke my leg the day before yesterday. I went to the hospital and they put on a cast.
c. I sprained my ankle yesterday. My friend Bob took me to the doctor, and she put on a bandage.
d. A dog bit me the other day. It didn't hurt very much, but I had to go to the doctor and get a shot.
e. I burned my hand on the stove this morning. My mother put on a bandage.
f. I fell off my bike on my way home from school. It hurts a little, but I'll be all right.

2 ► Listen to the conversation.
► Imagine you had one of the accidents in exercise 1. Act out a similar conversation with a partner.

A What's the matter?
B I broke my leg.
A I'd better go call for help. Stay here.

> **Some recommendations**
>
> I'd better . . .
> go call for help.
> get a doctor.
> put on a bandage.

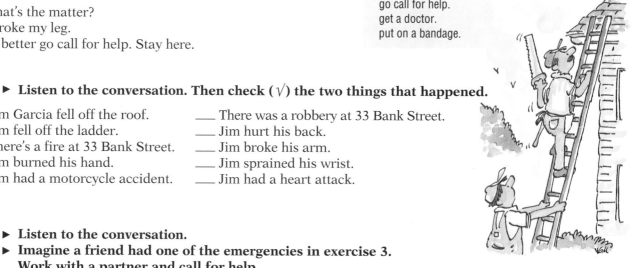

3 ► Listen to the conversation. Then check (√) the two things that happened.

___ Jim Garcia fell off the roof.
___ Jim fell off the ladder.
___ There's a fire at 33 Bank Street.
___ Jim burned his hand.
___ Jim had a motorcycle accident.
___ There was a robbery at 33 Bank Street.
___ Jim hurt his back.
___ Jim broke his arm.
___ Jim sprained his wrist.
___ Jim had a heart attack.

4 ► Listen to the conversation.
► Imagine a friend had one of the emergencies in exercise 3. Work with a partner and call for help.

Operator 911.
Mike My friend just fell off a ladder. Could you send an ambulance?
Operator Could I have your name, please?
Mike Yes, it's Michael Trent.
Operator And where's the emergency?
Mike At 33 Bank Street.
Operator All right, Mr. Trent. Stay calm. We'll send an ambulance right away.

> **Things you might need in an emergency**
>
> Could you send . . .
> a fire truck?
> an ambulance?
> a police car?

5 ▶ **Listen to the two possible conversations.**
▶ **Imagine you had one of the accidents in exercise 3. Have a similar conversation with a partner.**

A Hey, what happened to you?
B I sprained my ankle.
A When did it happen?
B The day before yesterday.
A Did you have to go to the hospital?

B Yes, I did.   **B** No, I didn't.

Some expressions of past time
yesterday
the day before yesterday
last week/month/year
two weeks/months/years ago

6 ▶ **Study the frame: The simple past tense**

Yes-no questions				Short answers		
Did	you he she we they	**have**	to go to the hospital?	Yes,	I he she	**did.**
				No,	we they	**didn't**.

7 ▶ **Complete the conversations with the correct forms of the simple past tense.**
▶ **Listen to check your work.**
▶ **Practice the conversations with a partner.**

1. John went skiing last weekend and broke his ankle. A friend sees him and thinks he broke his leg. What does the friend ask John?

   Friend _____ your leg?
   John No, _____. _____.

2. The Duponts just moved to California, and they sold their house in New York. Two neighbors are talking about them. What do they say?

   Neighbor 1 Did you hear? The Duponts moved to California.
   Neighbor 2 Really? _____ their house?
   Neighbor 1 Yes, _____. A very nice family bought it.

3. Mary usually goes to Thailand on vacation, but this year she went to South Korea. Mary's mother and a friend are talking. What do they say?

   Mother Mary had a wonderful vacation again this year.
   Friend _____ to Thailand again?
   Mother No, _____. _____.

4. Betty Smith came back from lunch and found a message. Mr. Jones wants Betty to call him back immediately. What does Betty's secretary ask an hour later?

   Secretary _____ Mr. Jones?
   Betty Yes, _____, but no one answered.

8 ▶ **Talk to your classmates. Work in groups. Give a brief description of an emergency you had or saw. Answer your classmates' questions.**

51. Did you have a good weekend?

1 ▶ **Listen to these statements. Match each statement with the picture it describes.**

___ 1. I went hiking.
___ 2. We went biking.
___ 3. I went fishing.
___ 4. We went camping.
___ 5. We went skiing.
___ 6. We visited my mother-in-law.
___ 7. I didn't go anywhere.
     I stayed home.
___ 8. I moved into a new apartment.

2 ▶ **Listen to the conversation.**
  ▶ **Act out similar conversations with a partner. Use the**
    examples in exercise 1 or your own information.

A Did you have a good weekend?
B It wasn't bad.
A What did you do?
B I went camping. What did you do?
A I didn't do anything special. I stayed
   home and worked around the house.

My weekend was . . .	My weekend wasn't . . .
pretty good.	bad.
nice.	great.
relaxing.	too good.
so-so.	much fun.

TALK ABOUT PAST ACTIVITIES • REVIEW: THE SIMPLE PAST TENSE OF IRREGULAR VERBS

3 ▸ **Study the frames.**

Review of the simple past tense: Irregular verbs		
I	**went** **didn't go**	biking in the mountains.
He	**flew** **didn't fly**	to Paris.
They	**had** **didn't have**	a good time.

Simple past tense of some irregular verbs								
bite	**bit**	drive	**drove**	hear	**heard**	run	**ran**
break	**broke**	fall	**fell**	hit	**hit**	say	**said**
bring	**brought**	feel	**felt**	hurt	**hurt**	see	**saw**
buy	**bought**	get	**got**	leave	**left**	sell	**sold**
catch	**caught**	give	**gave**	lose	**lost**	send	**sent**
come	**came**	go	**went**	make	**made**	take	**took**
cut	**cut**	grow	**grew**	meet	**met**	tell	**told**
do	**did**	have	**had**	put	**put**	think	**thought**

See p. 85 for a complete list of irregular verbs.

4 ▸ **Listen to the telephone conversation. Check the travel itinerary the people are talking about.**

Wednesday, July 17   arrive in Paris
Sunday, July 21   fly to Geneva
Monday, July 22   meet Franz and Helga
Wednesday, July 24   fly home

☐

Wednesday, July 17   arrive in Paris
Saturday, July 20 –
Sunday, July 21   drive to Geneva
Monday, July 22   meet Franz and Helga
Wednesday, July 24   start trip

☐

5 ▸ **Complete the captions with the simple past tense of the verbs in parentheses.**

1. Franz _____ the sandwich, but he _____ the ant. (eat)

2. We _____ all day, but we _____ at night. (ride)

3. Helga _____ the hat, but she _____ the shorts. (buy)

4. We _____ Mont Blanc, but we _____ the Matterhorn. (see)

6 ▸ **Interview a classmate. Find out if he or she had a good weekend. If it was good, find out what your classmate did. If it wasn't good, find out why.**

52. At least you weren't bored.

Steve drops by Charley's apartment one evening after work.

1

Steve Hey, what happened to our best player? We missed you at the game last night. Were you sick or something?

Charley No. I was really tired after work. I tried to call you, but your line was busy. How was the game?

Steve We lost. It wasn't your fault, though. We just didn't play well.

Charley Well, I'll be there next time. By the way, I heard your ad on the radio. It sounds good.

Steve Thanks. But you know, someone heard it and brought in a '49 Peugeot.

Charley A '49 Peugeot? I didn't know that model was still around.

Steve Neither did I. The engine was making a funny noise, and I worked on it for half an hour, but I couldn't fix it.

Charley But your ad says you can fix anything!

Steve I know. The guy with the Peugeot said the same thing. I really felt like an idiot.

Charley It sounds like you had a rough day. But at least you weren't bored. Nothing interesting ever happens at the bank.

Steve No? Are you looking for a new job?

Charley Not yet, but I'm going to start looking soon.

2. Figure it out

Say *True*, *False*, **or** *It doesn't say.*

1. Charley missed the game because he was sick.
2. Steve was on the phone with his mother when Charley tried to call.
3. The team didn't play well, and they lost the game.
4. Steve can fix anything.
5. Steve felt like an idiot when he couldn't fix the 1949 Peugeot.
6. Charley would like a more interesting job.

3. Your turn

As Steve and Charley are talking, Charley notices Steve's sprained wrist. Act out the conversation.

Charley	_____
Steve	I sprained my wrist.
Charley	_____
Steve	Last night, at the soccer game.
Charley	_____
Steve	No, I didn't. It wasn't serious enough for the hospital.
Charley	_____
Steve	Yeah, my mom took care of it. She's my favorite doctor. By the way, how was your weekend?
Charley	_____
Steve	What did you do?
Charley	_____

4. How to say it

Practice the conversation.

A How was your weekend?

B It wasn't bad. I didn't do anything special.

A Did you work?

B No, I didn't.

5. Listen in

While Steve and Charley are talking, a police story is on television. Read the questions below. Then listen to the conversation and choose *a* or *b*.

1. Where's the emergency?
   a. On 18th Street.
   b. On 19th Street.

2. What's the problem?
   a. Some people are fighting.
   b. There's a fire.

3. What's the woman's name?
   a. Alice.
   b. She didn't tell the police officer her name.

53. RESCUE

For centuries, people have climbed mountains—Kilimanjaro in Tanzania, Fuji in Japan, Everest between Nepal and China. They have climbed for religious reasons, for reasons of survival, or just because they were curious. The actual "sport" of mountain climbing was probably invented over 200 years ago at Mont Blanc in the French Alps. Mountain climbing can be a challenging sport, but it is not without danger and accidents. The following is an account of a rescue from Mont Blanc by the brave members of the Peloton de Gendarmerie de Haute Montagne (Mountain Rescue Squad), a division of the French police.

I had looked forward to this day for a long time. Finally I, Kirsty Stuart, would stand on the top of Mont Blanc, the highest mountain in Europe. Although I climbed often in my native Scotland, this was my first trip to the Alps. My companions—Jean-Pierre Barton, Maurice Gautier, and Mary Sargent—and I left our camp at the bottom of the mountain early and planned to reach the summit by late morning. The snow was hard and we made good time.

As we neared the top, large clouds gathered and it began to snow. We found shelter and decided to wait for the snow to stop. After three hours, however, we decided to go back and try again the next day. We started down the mountain in the thick snow. Jean-Pierre forgot his sunglasses and went back to look for them. As he was returning to us, he started to fall. "Look out below!" he called.

His fall started an avalanche and it was falling towards us! I was swept away by the heavy snow and landed several meters below. Jean-Pierre hurried down to me. "Are you O.K.?" he asked as he brushed the snow off me.

"I think I broke my leg," I answered.

"I'd better radio for help!" he said. "Where are the others?" We couldn't see Maurice or Mary anywhere.

Jean-Pierre called the emergency radio number, and the police said they would send help right away. It seemed like hours, but only minutes later we heard the welcome sound of a helicopter. Jean-Pierre waved his bright orange jacket in the air. The helicopter couldn't land on the mountainside, so they lowered two men, two dogs, and a stretcher. One man ran to me, but I told him to search for the others. The dogs were trained for avalanche rescue and soon began to dig frantically in the snow. "They've found them!" Jean-Pierre called.

Bernardo, the lead dog, found Mary's scarf and led the rescuers to her. Maurice was nearby. The men gave us hot drinks and warm blankets and then prepared to lift us into the helicopter. Two men inside the helicopter pulled us up by the ropes. I went first on the stretcher.

Once we were safely inside, the helicopter flew to the hospital in Chamonix. Our poor rescuers and their dogs had to climb all the way back down the mountain. Later we would find these brave men and thank them for saving our lives.

1. Read the magazine article. Then scan the article and find:

a. how many climbers there were.
b. the name of the mountain they tried to climb.
c. how many rescuers there were.
d. the location of the hospital.

2. Discuss these questions.

1. How did the avalanche start?
2. Who found Mary Sargent?
3. Would you like to go mountain climbing? Why or why not?

PREVIEW

FUNCTIONS/THEMES	LANGUAGE	FORMS
Get to know someone	Where are you from originally? I'm from Argentina. How long have you lived in New York? I've been here for five years. I've been here since 1990.	The present perfect: information questions and statements *For* and *since*
Keep a conversation going Talk about abilities	So, you're from Argentina. Uh-huh. I'd like to go to South America someday. Do you know how to speak Spanish? A little. Where did you learn it? I studied it in school.	*Know how to*
Give someone a message	Did anyone call? Yes. Someone named Sharon Kennedy. What did she want? She wants you to call her back at work.	Object pronouns: *me, you, him, her, us, them* Direct and indirect objects
Instruct someone politely	Someone ordered these sandwiches. Could you give them to the woman over there? Sure.	*Could*
Get the correct change	Excuse me. I think I gave you a twenty. Oh, then I owe you ten dollars. I'm very sorry.	

Preview the conversations.

These two people don't know each other. However, they feel free to talk to each other because they have something in common: they like the same music. Is it acceptable in your country to strike up a conversation with a stranger when you notice that you both have things in common?

54. I really need a break.

Luis is a cashier at Endicott Booksellers in New York City. He is having a busy day.

A

Luis Hello. Endicott Booksellers.
Sharon I'd like to speak to Marcia, please.
Luis Marcia's at lunch. Can I take a message?
Sharon Yes. Please tell her that Sharon Kennedy called, and ask her to call me back at work. She has the number.
Luis O.K. I'll give her the message.

B

Delivery man Hi. I'm from Ralph's Coffee Shop. Somebody ordered these sandwiches.
Luis Oh, right. Could you give them to the woman over there? She ordered them.
Delivery man Sure.

C

Luis José Luis Rodríguez—El Puma. You chose a good CD.
Customer Do you think so?
Luis Yes. He wrote all the lyrics and they're really beautiful.
Customer Oh, can you speak Spanish?
Luis Yes, I speak it fluently. It was my first language.
Customer Where are you from originally?
Luis Well, I was born in Venezuela.
Customer Really? How long have you lived in New York?
Luis Oh, I grew up here. I've been in New York since I was ten.
Customer I'd like to go to South America someday.
Luis Would you?
Customer Yeah. I imagine it's very interesting.
Luis Do you know how to speak Spanish?
Customer Not very well, but I'm learning. I speak Portuguese, though.
Luis Oh? Where did you learn Portuguese?
Customer I studied it in college.
Luis Well, then maybe Spanish will be easy for you.
Customer I hope so, but they're very different languages.
Luis So, that's $8.95 . . . and here's your change.
Customer Excuse me. I think I gave you a twenty.
Luis Oh, then I owe you ten dollars. I'm very sorry.
Customer No problem.

Marcia Hi, Luis. I'm back. Did anyone call?
Luis Yes. Someone named Sharon Kennedy.
Marcia What did she want?
Luis She wants you to call her back at work.
Marcia Anyone else?
Luis No, that's all.
Marcia O.K. Did you have lunch?
Luis No, I didn't have time. I was too busy.
Marcia Why don't you go out now? I'll take over for you.
Luis Thanks a lot. I really need a break.

Figure it out

1. Listen to the conversations and choose *a*, *b*, or *c*.

1. a. Luis speaks Spanish.
   b. The customer speaks Spanish.
   c. Both Luis and the customer speak Spanish.

2. a. First, Luis gives the customer the right change.
   b. First, Luis gives the customer the wrong change.
   c. First, Luis gives the customer no change.

2. Listen again. Say *True, False*, or *It doesn't say*.

1. The sandwiches from the coffee shop are for Luis.
2. Endicott Booksellers sells books and CDs only in English.
3. Luis was born in South America.
4. Luis has lived in New York since he was 10 years old.
5. The customer often travels to South America.
6. Luis took a telephone message for Marcia.
7. Marcia doesn't have time to call Sharon back.
8. Luis is tired.

3. Find another way to say it.

1. That's O.K.   *No problem.*
2. Can you speak Spanish?
3. You should go out now.
4. I'll take your place.
5. I need a rest.

55. Where are you from originally?

1 ► **Listen to the conversation and complete the information about each person.**

1. _____ is from Kenya originally. He has lived in New York for _____ years.

2. _____ grew up in Washington. She has lived in New York since _____ .

3. _____ is originally from Japan. She has lived in New York since _____ .

4. _____ is from Argentina originally. He has lived in New York for _____ years.

Magumi · Abdul · Aldo · Dee

2 ► **Listen to the conversation.**
► **Practice the conversation with a partner. Use your own information.**

A Where are you from originally?
B I'm from Argentina.
A How long have you lived in New York?
B I've been here for five years.

> Use *for* with a period of time.
> Use *since* with a specific time or date.
>
> I've been here . . .
>
> | for two months. | since 1990. |
> | for five years. | since October. |
> | for a long time. | since I was 10. |

3 ► **Study the frames: The present perfect**

Information questions

| How long | have | you we they | lived been | in New York? |
| | has | he she | | |

Affirmative and negative statements

| I We You They | have ('ve) haven't | lived been | here for ten years. here very long. |
| He She | has ('s) hasn't | lived been | here since October. here very long. |

Base form	Simple past	Past participle
be	was, were	**been***
live	lived	**lived**
work	worked	**worked**

*See p. 166 for the past participles of irregular verbs.

4 ► **Complete this article from an employee newsletter. Use the present perfect of the verbs in parentheses.**

This week our spotlight is on Magumi Saito, the new manager of our Far East department. Ms. Saito is originally from Kyoto. She _____ (not be) in New York very long. In fact, she _____ (be) here for only two months, but she _____ (live) in the United States since 1990, when she attended Boston University. She _____ (work) for Danton Bookstores for one year, first in Boston and now in New York. Ms. Saito holds a master's degree in international business and says she _____ (be) interested in the book business for a long time. She is also a collector of old books. And how long _____ she _____ (collect) books? "I _____ (collect) books since I was a child," Ms. Saito reports.

5 ▶ Listen to two ways to continue the conversation in exercise 2.
  ▶ Act out a similar conversation with a partner.

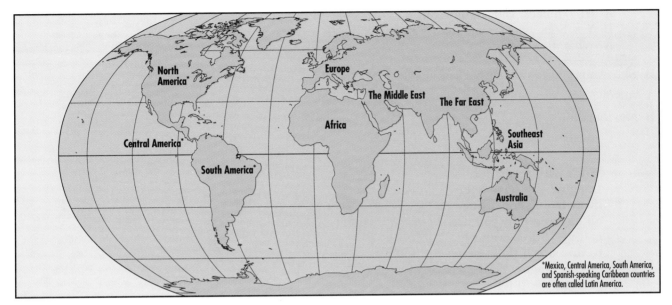

Mexico, Central America, South America, and Spanish-speaking Caribbean countries are often called Latin America.

A So, you're from Argentina.
B Uh-huh.

A I'd like to go to South America someday.
B Would you?
A Yeah. I imagine it's very interesting.
B Do you know how to speak Spanish?

A A little.

B Where did you learn it?
A I studied it in school.

A I've been to Argentina.
B Really? How did you like it?
A It was very interesting.
B Do you know how to speak Spanish?

A No, I don't. Unfortunately, I'm not very good at languages.

Do you know how to speak . . .?

Yes, I speak it fluently.
We spoke it at home.
A little.
I studied it in school.
Not very well.
A friend taught me.
No, I don't.
I'm not very good at languages.

6 ▶ Listen to the continuation of the conversation from exercise 5. Check (√) the things Aldo and Magumi like and know how to do.

Languages	English	Spanish	Japanese	Music	Spanish music	American music	Japanese music	Musical Instruments	The piano	The guitar	The violin	Sports	Play tennis	Swim	Ski
Aldo knows how to speak				Aldo likes				Aldo can play				Aldo knows how to			
Magumi knows how to speak				Magumi likes				Magumi can play				Magumi knows how to			

7 ▶ Find out where a classmate is from originally, and find out how long he or she has been in this city. Use your imagination and keep the conversation going.

56. Did anyone call?

GIVE SOMEONE A MESSAGE • OBJECT PRONOUNS • DIRECT AND INDIRECT OBJECTS

1
- ▶ **Listen to the two possible conversations.**
- ▶ **Practice the conversations with a partner.**

A Hi, I'm back. Did anyone call?
B Yes. Someone named Sharon Kennedy.
A What did she want?

B She wants you to call her back at work.
A Anyone else?
B No, that's all.

B She didn't leave a message.
A Anyone else?
B No, that's all.

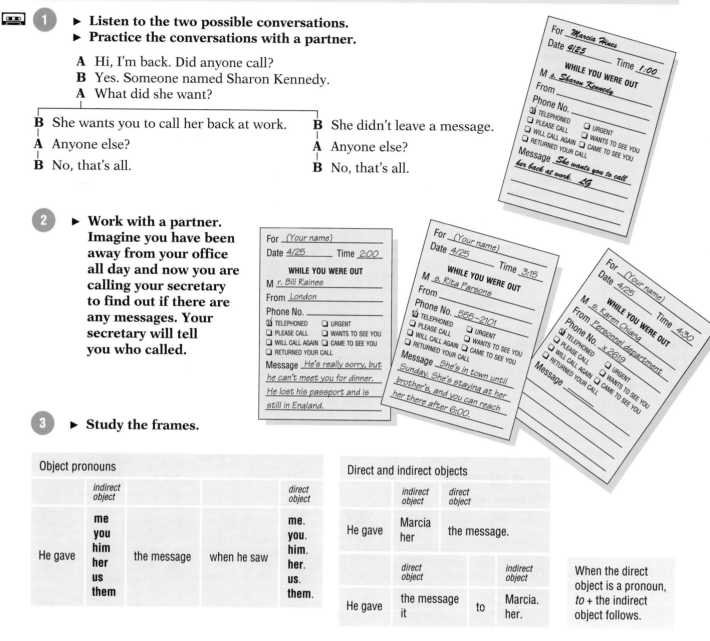

For _Marcia Hines_
Date _4/25_   Time _1:00_
WHILE YOU WERE OUT
M _s. Sharon Kennedy_
From _____
Phone No. _____
☑ TELEPHONED
☐ PLEASE CALL   ☐ URGENT
☐ WILL CALL AGAIN   ☐ WANTS TO SEE YOU
☐ RETURNED YOUR CALL ☐ CAME TO SEE YOU
Message _She wants you to call her back at work. LG_

2
- ▶ **Work with a partner. Imagine you have been away from your office all day and now you are calling your secretary to find out if there are any messages. Your secretary will tell you who called.**

For _(Your name)_
Date _4/25_   Time _2:00_
WHILE YOU WERE OUT
M _r. Bill Raines_
From _London_
Phone No. _____
☑ TELEPHONED   ☐ URGENT
☐ PLEASE CALL   ☐ WANTS TO SEE YOU
☐ WILL CALL AGAIN   ☐ CAME TO SEE YOU
☐ RETURNED YOUR CALL
Message _He's really sorry, but he can't meet you for dinner. He lost his passport and is still in England._

For _(Your name)_
Date _4/25_   Time _3:15_
WHILE YOU WERE OUT
M _s. Rita Parsons_
From _____
Phone No. _555-2101_
☑ TELEPHONED
☐ PLEASE CALL   ☐ URGENT
☐ WILL CALL AGAIN   ☐ WANTS TO SEE YOU
☐ RETURNED YOUR CALL ☐ CAME TO SEE YOU
Message _She's in town until Sunday. She's staying at her brother's, and you can reach her there after 6:00._

For _(Your name)_
Date _4/25_   Time _4:30_
WHILE YOU WERE OUT
M _s. Karen Chiang_
From _Personnel department_
Phone No. _x 2619_
☑ TELEPHONED
☐ PLEASE CALL   ☐ URGENT
☐ WILL CALL AGAIN   ☐ WANTS TO SEE YOU
☐ RETURNED YOUR CALL ☐ CAME TO SEE YOU
Message _____

3
- ▶ **Study the frames.**

Object pronouns

	indirect object			*direct object*
He gave	me you him her us them	the message	when he saw	me. you. him. her. us. them.

Direct and indirect objects

	indirect object	*direct object*
He gave	Marcia her	the message.

	direct object		*indirect object*
He gave	the message it	to	Marcia. her.

When the direct object is a pronoun, *to* + the indirect object follows.

4
- ▶ **Jim and Alice work together. Complete their conversations, using direct and indirect objects.**
- ▶ **Listen to check your work.**
- ▶ **Practice the conversations with a partner.**

1. **Man** Can I speak to Jim, please?
   Alice He isn't here right now. Can I _give him a message_?
   Man Yes. Could you tell him Jack called?
   Alice Sure.

2. **Jim** Alice, could you give this book to Mr. Wilson?
   Alice I already did. _____ last week.
   Jim Oh, thanks. You remember everything.

3. **Alice** There's a message from Stan and Marcy Miller. Do you know them?
   Jim Of course. _____ .
   Alice The Millers bought your old house? I didn't know that.

4. **Alice** Oh, look. Your friend Jack left his gloves here.
   Jim No problem. We're going to the gym together later, so I'll _____ .

57. I think I gave you a twenty.

INSTRUCT SOMEONE POLITELY • *COULD*

1 ▶ **Complete the conversations with polite instructions. Use the instructions in the box.**
   ▶ **Listen to check your work.**
   ▶ **Practice the conversations with a partner.**

> Take it to the Lost and Found.
> Put it in an envelope and save it.
> Give them to him tomorrow.
> Give them to the woman over there.

1. **A** Someone ordered these sandwiches.
   B *Could you give them to the woman over there?*
   A Sure.

2. **A** Someone left some change by the cash register.
   B _____
   A O.K. I'm sure someone will come back for it.

3. **A** Someone left a wallet here.
   B _____
   A O.K.

4. **A** Your assistant went home and forgot these.
   B _____
   A All right. I'll put them in my desk.

GET THE CORRECT CHANGE

2 ▶ **Listen to the conversation between a cashier and a customer. Then choose *a* or *b*.**

1. The customer bought
   a. a book.
   b. some photographs.

2. The customer wants the cashier
   a. to put them in a bag.
   b. to put it in a box.

3. The customer
   a. paid cash for his purchase.
   b. charged his purchase.

4. The customer gave the cashier
   a. a twenty-dollar bill.
   b. a fifty-dollar bill.

3 ▶ **Listen to the conversation.**
   ▶ **Act out a similar conversation with a partner. Use the information in the table.**

Cashier So, that's $8.95. And here's your change.
Customer Excuse me. I think I gave you a twenty.
Cashier Oh, then I owe you ten dollars. I'm very sorry.
Customer No problem.

The price is:	You gave the cashier:	The cashier gave you:
$ 8.95	$20.00	$1.05
$ 6.95	$20.00	$3.05
$ 3.69	$10.00	$1.31
$19.95	$50.00	$ .05

58. Do you speak Hungarian?

Emma Kovacs and Tom Anderson are at the Hollywood Bowl, a large outdoor theater in Los Angeles. They're going to see an Italian opera.

1

Tom It certainly is beautiful here.

Emma It really is. Oh, look. Peter Kadar is singing tonight.

Tom I don't think I've ever heard of him.

Emma He's a well-known Hungarian singer, and he performs in the U.S. every year. I'm always interested in Hungarian performers. My parents were both musicians from Hungary.

Tom Oh, is Kovacs a Hungarian name?

Emma Well, Kovacs is my married name. But, yes, my husband was Hungarian, too.

Tom That's interesting. Do you speak Hungarian?

Emma Yes, we spoke it at home when I was a child. I also spoke it with my husband from time to time.

Tom My parents came here from Sweden, so I speak a little Swedish, but I didn't marry a Swedish woman. In fact, I've never been married.

Emma Well, airline pilots travel a lot, so I suppose it's hard to have a family.

Tom Not really. Most airline pilots get married. I just never wanted to settle down.

Emma I can understand that. I got married right after I finished medical school, and I never had a free moment after that.

Tom A doctor's life must be very hard.

Emma Well, sometimes it is. . . . Look, here comes the conductor.

2. Figure it out

Say *True, False,* or *It doesn't say.*

1. One of the opera singers is Hungarian.
2. Emma learned to speak Hungarian from her parents.
3. Emma's husband spoke Hungarian.
4. Emma's children speak Hungarian.
5. Tom speaks Swedish fluently.
6. Tom didn't get married because he didn't have time for a family.
7. Emma got married before she went to medical school.

3. Listen in

Look at the people in the audience below. Then
listen to the conversations and match each
conversation with the appropriate people.

Conversation 1   a
Conversation 2   b
Conversation 3   c

4. How to say it

Practice the phrase below. Then practice
the conversation.

did you   [dɪdʒu]

A Where did you learn Japanese?
B I lived in Japan for two years.
A Did you study it before you went there?
B Yes. I studied it in college.

5. Your turn

Two musicians, Andrea Lanza and Mark Crespi, are talking to each other before the
opera begins. Mark is a new member of the orchestra. Take the role of Andrea or
Mark and act out the conversation. Use this information.

Andrea was born in Brazil but grew up in Miami. She spoke English at home with her parents.	Mark's from Los Angeles, but his parents are from Italy. He spoke Italian at home with them.
Andrea asks if Mark understands Italian.	Mark says he speaks it fluently.
She asks where he learned Italian.	He says where he learned Italian.
She says she'd like to go to Italy someday.	He asks where Andrea is from.
She says where she's from.	He asks if she speaks Portuguese.
She tells why she forgot all her Portuguese.	

59. 🔊

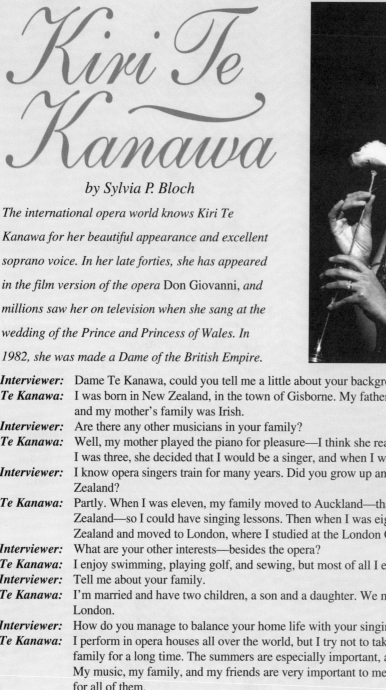

Kiri Te Kanawa

by Sylvia P. Bloch

The international opera world knows Kiri Te Kanawa for her beautiful appearance and excellent soprano voice. In her late forties, she has appeared in the film version of the opera Don Giovanni, *and millions saw her on television when she sang at the wedding of the Prince and Princess of Wales. In 1982, she was made a Dame of the British Empire.*

Interviewer: Dame Te Kanawa, could you tell me a little about your background?

Te Kanawa: I was born in New Zealand, in the town of Gisborne. My father was Maori, a native Polynesian, and my mother's family was Irish.

Interviewer: Are there any other musicians in your family?

Te Kanawa: Well, my mother played the piano for pleasure—I think she really wanted to be a performer. When I was three, she decided that I would be a singer, and when I was seven, I started playing the piano.

Interviewer: I know opera singers train for many years. Did you grow up and receive your training in New Zealand?

Te Kanawa: Partly. When I was eleven, my family moved to Auckland—that's the largest city in New Zealand—so I could have singing lessons. Then when I was eighteen, my mother and I left New Zealand and moved to London, where I studied at the London Opera Centre.

Interviewer: What are your other interests—besides the opera?

Te Kanawa: I enjoy swimming, playing golf, and sewing, but most of all I enjoy spending time with my family.

Interviewer: Tell me about your family.

Te Kanawa: I'm married and have two children, a son and a daughter. We make our home in Surrey, near London.

Interviewer: How do you manage to balance your home life with your singing career?

Te Kanawa: I perform in opera houses all over the world, but I try not to take jobs that keep me away from my family for a long time. The summers are especially important, and we take the children to Portugal. My music, my family, and my friends are very important to me. I do everything I can to have time for all of them.

1. Read the interview and answer the questions.

1. What does Dame Kiri Te Kanawa do for a living?
2. Where is she from originally?
3. How long has she lived in England?
4. What are her interests besides the opera?

2. The interview above is not a real interview. The author only imagined talking to Kiri Te Kanawa. Imagine you are planning to interview a famous person. Who will you interview, and what questions will you ask?

P R E V I E W

FUNCTIONS/THEMES	LANGUAGE	FORMS
Talk about plans	Will you be around this summer? Yes, I will. I've got a job at the YMCA. Maybe I'll take summer classes. I'll probably take summer classes.	The future with *will*: information questions; statements; yes-no questions and short answers *Maybe* and *probably*
Wish someone well	Have a good summer. Thanks. You too. And good luck on your interview. Thanks. I'll need it.	
Ask for and give directions	Excuse me. How far is the National Theater from here? About three blocks. How do I get there? Walk down F Street to Fourteenth Street and turn right. Is this the way to the personnel office? Yes, it is. Go down the hall and to the right.	
Thank someone	Thank you very much. My pleasure.	
Interview for a job	I'm looking for a summer job. Are you interested in working full time? Yes, I am.	Preposition + gerund
Talk about school	Where do you go to school? I go to George Washington University. When will you graduate? Next June.	
Talk about skills and interests	Do you have any special skills or interests? Well, I can use a computer and I know how to speak Spanish. And in my free time, I like to read.	

Preview the conversations.

American colleges and universities often have students from other cities, states, and countries. During the long summer vacation, most of these students go home, but some stay and get jobs. How do students in your country spend their school vacations?

60. Interview

 Meg Harper and Jim Cruz are students at George Washington University in Washington, D.C. Today is the last day before summer vacation.

A

Meg Will you be around this summer, Jim?

Jim No, I won't. I'm going to spend the summer at home with my parents.

Meg Where's that?

Jim New Orleans. What are you going to do?

Meg I'm not sure yet. I've got an interview at the *Washington Post* at one today, so maybe I'll get a job there.

Jim Oh, yeah? That sounds interesting.

Meg Yeah. I'm keeping my fingers crossed.

Jim Well, I probably won't see you before I leave, so have a good summer.

Meg Thanks. You too.

Jim And good luck on your interview.

Meg Thanks. I'll need it.

B

Meg Excuse me. How far is Fifteenth Street from here? I'm looking for the *Washington Post*.

Man About two blocks. It's between Vermont Avenue and Sixteenth Street.

Meg Thanks a lot.

Man My pleasure.

C

Meg Excuse me. Is this the way to the personnel department?

Woman Yes, it is. Go down the hall and to the right. It's across from the cafeteria.

Meg Thank you.

D

Mr. Reed So, you're looking for a summer job. Are you interested in working full time?
Meg Yes, I am.
Mr. Reed And where do you go to school?
Meg George Washington University.
Mr. Reed Oh, yes. I see that on your application. When will you graduate?
Meg Next June. I only have one more year.
Mr. Reed Do you have any special skills or interests?
Meg Well, I can use a computer and I know how to speak Spanish. And in my free time, I like to read.

E

Meg Thank you very much, Mr. Reed. I'm really excited about the job.
Mr. Reed Well, I think you'll enjoy working for the *Post*.

Figure it out

1. Listen to the conversations. Then choose *a* or *b*.

1. This summer Jim is going to
   a. stay in Washington, D.C.
   b. go home.

2. This summer Meg is going to
   a. work at the *Washington Post*.
   b. take classes at George Washington University.

2. Listen again and say *True, False,* or *It doesn't say*.

1. Jim's parents live in Washington, D.C.
2. Jim is going to work this summer.
3. The *Washington Post* is on Fifteenth Street.
4. The personnel department is on the second floor.
5. Meg wants to work all year.
6. Meg is going to be a reporter at the *Washington Post*.

3. Match.

1. Will you be around this summer?
2. What are you going to do?
3. Good luck on your interview.
4. How far is Fifteenth Street from here?
5. Where do you go to school?
6. When will you graduate?

a. No, I won't.
b. About two blocks.
c. Next June.
d. George Washington University.
e. Thanks. I'll need it.
f. I'm not sure yet.

61. Will you be around this summer?

TALK ABOUT PLANS • THE FUTURE WITH *WILL* • *MAYBE* AND *PROBABLY*

1 ▶ **Sam, Pam, Andy, Sue, and Bob are university students. What are they going to do during their summer vacation? Listen and then complete the sentences with the name of the correct person.**

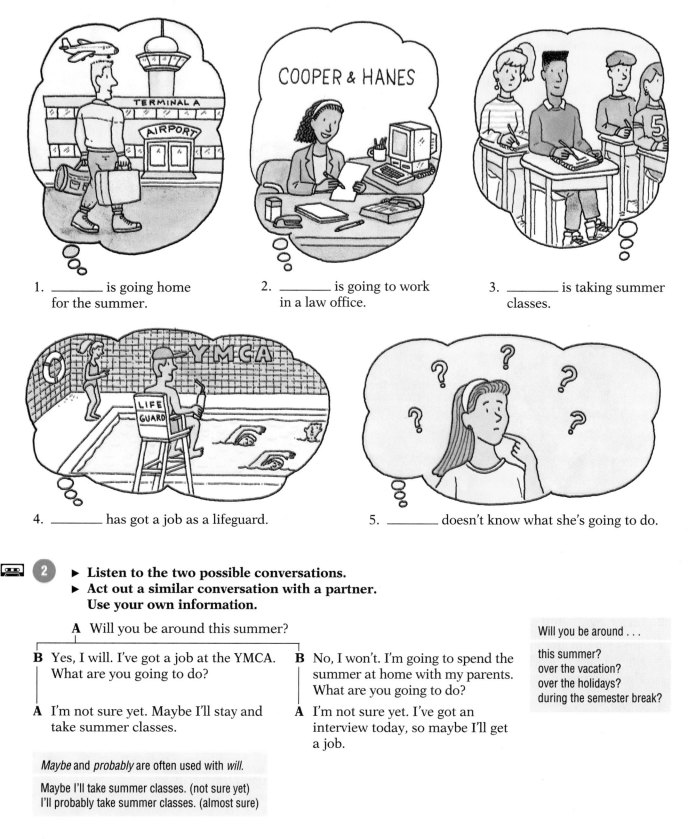

1. _____ is going home for the summer.

2. _____ is going to work in a law office.

3. _____ is taking summer classes.

4. _____ has got a job as a lifeguard.

5. _____ doesn't know what she's going to do.

2 ▶ **Listen to the two possible conversations.**
▶ **Act out a similar conversation with a partner. Use your own information.**

A Will you be around this summer?

B Yes, I will. I've got a job at the YMCA. What are you going to do?

A I'm not sure yet. Maybe I'll stay and take summer classes.

B No, I won't. I'm going to spend the summer at home with my parents. What are you going to do?

A I'm not sure yet. I've got an interview today, so maybe I'll get a job.

> Will you be around . . .
>
> this summer?
> over the vacation?
> over the holidays?
> during the semester break?

Maybe and *probably* are often used with *will*.

Maybe I'll take summer classes. (not sure yet)
I'll probably take summer classes. (almost sure)

3 ▶ **Listen to the rest of the second conversation in exercise 2.**
▶ **Imagine you are leaving for vacation. Wish your partner well.**

B Well, I probably won't see you before I leave, so have a good summer.
A Thanks. You too.
B And good luck on your interview.
A Thanks. I'll need it.

Have a good . . .	And good luck on your . . .
summer.	interview.
vacation.	test.
trip.	job.

4 ▶ **Study the frames: The future with *will***

Information questions				Affirmative and negative statements		
When	will	you she it we they	be there?	I She It We They	**will ('ll)**	**be** there tomorrow.
					will not (won't)	**be** there until late.

Yes-no questions	Short answers
Will you **be** here tomorrow?	Yes, I **will**. No, I **won't**.

5 ▶ **Complete the conversation with *will* and the verbs in parentheses.**
▶ **Listen to check your work.**
▶ **Practice the conversation with a partner.**

A I think I _____ (go) to Boston during the break. Why don't you come along?
B Oh, I don't know. Where _____ (stay)?
A We _____ (find) a cheap hotel somewhere.
B I _____ (have to) think about it. When do you need to know?
A Sometime this weekend.
B O.K. I _____ (call) you.
A I _____ (not be) home tomorrow during the day, but I _____ (be) here tomorrow night.
B _____ (be) home on Sunday?
A Yes.
B Good. I _____ (call) you then. I have three final exams next week, so I _____ (be) at the library all day tomorrow and I probably _____ (not get) home until late.
A O.K. I_____ (talk) to you Sunday.
B Fine.

6 ▶ **Interview a classmate. Find out what he or she is going to do this summer or during the next school break. Tell your classmate what you are going to do.**

62. How far is Fifteenth Street from here?

ASK FOR AND GIVE DIRECTIONS • THANK SOMEONE

1 ▶ **Listen to the conversation.**
  ▶ **Act out a similar conversation with a partner.**

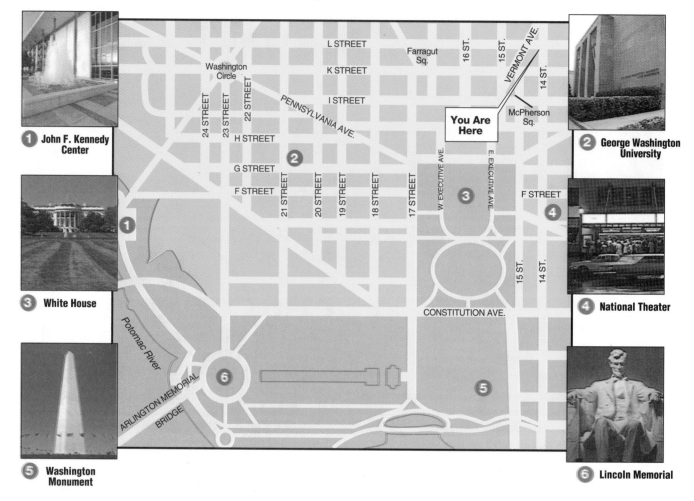

1 John F. Kennedy Center

2 George Washington University

3 White House

4 National Theater

5 Washington Monument

6 Lincoln Memorial

A Excuse me. How far is Fifteenth Street from here?
B About two blocks. (It's between Vermont Avenue and Sixteenth Street.)
A Thank you very much.
B My pleasure.

2 ▶ **Where is the man going? Listen to the directions and find the place on the map above.**

3 ▶ **Listen to the conversation.**
  ▶ **Imagine you are at the White House in Washington, D.C. Act out a similar conversation and ask for directions to one of the other places on the map.**

A Excuse me. How far is the National Theater from here?
B Oh, about three blocks.
A How do I get there?
B Walk down F Street to Fourteenth Street and turn right. Go straight ahead about a block, and it should be on your left.

63. Are you interested in working full time?

1
► Listen to the conversation.
► Imagine you are looking for one of the places at the *Washington Post*.
Act out a similar conversation with a partner.

A Excuse me. Is this the way to the personnel department?
B Yes, it is. Go down the hall and to the right. It's across from the cafeteria.
A Thank you.

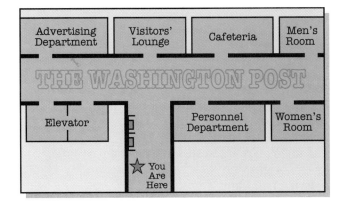

2
► Listen to the two conversations.
► Practice the conversations with a partner.

A I'm looking for a summer job.
B Are you interested in working full time?
A Yes, I am.
B And where do you go to school?
A I go to George Washington University.
B When will you graduate?
A Next June.
B Do you have any special skills or interests?
A Well, I can use a computer and I know how to speak Spanish. And in my free time, I like to read.

A I'm looking for a summer job.
B Are you interested in working full time?
A No, I'd like to work part time.
B And where do you go to school?
A I went to George Washington University.
B When did you graduate?
A In 1992.
B Do you have any special skills or interests?
A Well, I can use a computer and I know how to speak Spanish. And in my free time, I like to read.

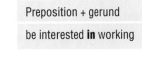

Preposition + gerund

be interested **in** working

3
► Another applicant is interviewing for a job. Listen to the interview and check (√) the appropriate items on the interviewer's checklist.

4
► Play these roles.

Student A You are the director of personnel for a small company. Use the Interviewer's Checklist above and interview Student B.

Student B You are in the personnel office of a small company and are applying for a job. Answer Student A's questions.

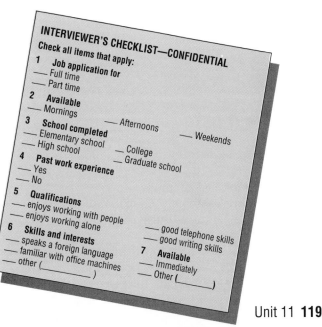

INTERVIEWER'S CHECKLIST—CONFIDENTIAL
Check all items that apply:
1 **Job application for**
— Full time
— Part time
2 **Available**
— Mornings
— Afternoons
— Weekends
3 **School completed**
— Elementary school
— High school
— College
— Graduate school
4 **Past work experience**
— Yes
— No
5 **Qualifications**
— enjoys working with people
— enjoys working alone
6 **Skills and interests**
— speaks a foreign language
— familiar with office machines
— other (_____)
— good telephone skills
— good writing skills
7 **Available**
— Immediately
— Other (_____)

64. How soon can you start?

Bonnie Perkins called Eva and told her there was an opening at Burger Ranch. Eva has an interview with Jan Souza, the manager of Burger Ranch.

Burger Ranch

Hamburger		$2.39
Cheeseburger		2.69
Chicken sandwich		3.19
Fish sandwich		3.49
Ranch salad		2.29
French fries	lg.	1.19
	sm.	.79

DRINKS

Coffee/Tea		.89
Milk		1.09
Soda	lg.	1.39
	sm.	.89
Milkshake		1.49

DESSERTS

Ranch chocolate chip cookie	.89
Apple pie	1.39

①

Jan Do you have any work experience, Eva?

Eva No, I've never had a job before.

Jan How old are you?

Eva Sixteen.

Jan You're interested in working part time, right?

Eva Yes, I am.

Jan Where do you go to school?

Eva I'm a junior at Susan B. Anthony High School.

Jan Oh, that's right. You and Bonnie go to the same school. Well, about the job—it gets very busy here in the evenings. You have to work fast, and there's a lot of pressure.

Eva That's no problem.

Jan I'm looking for someone dependable. Will you be here every afternoon at four?

Eva Oh, yes. I'm always on time.

Jan The hours are four to eight, Monday through Friday. You'll make five dollars an hour. How does that sound?

Eva That sounds fine.

Jan Oh, and you'll get a free meal every evening. Do you like hamburgers?

Eva I love them.

Jan Well, I think you'll like it here. How soon can you start?

Eva Can I start today?

Jan Today?

Eva Yeah. I mean, there's no rush. I'm just anxious to start.

Jan Well, first you have to get a uniform and some comfortable shoes. You can start tomorrow at four.

2. Figure it out

Say *True, False,* or *It doesn't say.*

1. Eva had a job last summer.
2. Bonnie told Eva about the job two days ago.
3. There's an opening at Burger Ranch on weekends.
4. Eva will probably have to work hard.
5. Eva's going to work twenty hours a week.
6. Eva will start her new job next week.

🔲 3. Listen in

The man below is asking for directions. Read the questions. Then listen to the conversation and answer the questions.

1. What street is Pacific Electronics on?
2. How far is Pacific Electronics from Burger Ranch?

🔲 4. How to say it

Practice the words below. Then practice the conversation.

I'll
you'll
he'll
we'll
they'll

A I'll be here tomorrow.
B What about Jim?
A He'll come around ten.
B And Bob and Sherry?
A They'll be here, too.
B Oh, then we'll all be here.
A You mean you'll be here, too?
B Of course.

5. Your turn

Eva runs into her friend Rick on her way home from Burger Ranch. She tells him about her new job. Act out the conversation.

Rick Hi, Eva.
Eva _____
Rick Fine. Listen, will you be around tomorrow after school?
Eva _____
Rick That's great! What are your hours?
Eva _____
Rick Is the pay good?
Eva _____
Rick Well, I have to go now. Good luck on your new job.
Eva _____

WHERE WILL WE GO FROM HERE?

In the twentieth century, many inventions brought quick and dramatic change to our lives. Consider, for example, the electric light. During the 1870s, two inventors, Joseph Swan in England and Thomas Edison in the United States, perfected their models of electric lamps. By December 1882, 203 customers in New York City were living and working by the light of 3,144 electric lamps. The distribution of electricity to the public led the way to many conveniences we take for granted in our homes today: the radio, the automatic washing machine, the air conditioner, and many others.

In 1903, the Wright brothers built and flew the first airplane with a motor. Their first flight lasted only 12 seconds and went only 120 feet (about 36 meters). By 1970, the Boeing 747 jumbo jet carried 350 people across the Atlantic Ocean from the United States to Europe in about 7 hours. In 1976, service started on the Concorde, a plane developed by the French and British that travels faster than the speed of sound. However, probably nothing about air travel can compare to an event in 1969: approximately 60 years after the first flight of an airplane, astronauts landed on the moon!

In addition to wanting to travel and learn more about the world, people wanted better and quicker communication with each other. The first telephone conversation was in 1876, when an American, Alexander Graham Bell, spoke on his invention to an assistant in another room. Today, telephones are everywhere —even in cars. We can speak to a single person or to many people at once. Soon we will be able to see the person we are talking to on video-telephones (some models are available now). We can already send pictures by phone using a fax machine, and we can even hook up computers to telephones in order to transfer information back and forth.

It took many years and many people to develop television technology, but by the 1950s, everyone was interested in owning a television set. In the 1960s, satellites made it possible for people to watch events happening across the globe. Since the 1970s, TVs have gotten bigger—and smaller. VCRs make it possible to record TV shows and watch them later, and video cameras give people the chance to make their own movies to watch. People even play video games on their TVs. It is amazing to realize that in less than 50 years from the early experiments with television, the "Live Aid" concert on TV in 1985 was watched by 1.5 billion people around the world.

About a hundred years ago the electric light, the telephone, the TV, and the airplane did not exist. These scientific developments have changed our lives in a very short time. As we enter the twenty-first century, we might wonder "Where will we go from here?"

1. **Look at the title of the magazine article and the pictures. What do you think the article is about?**

2. **Read the article. Then scan it and find at least ten things that did not exist about a century ago.**

3. **Discuss the question at the end of the last paragraph.**

Review of units 8–11

1 ▶ **Complete the paragraph with *when*, *as soon as*, *before*, and *after*.**

My name's Tom Chomsky and I live in Apartment 44. I usually lead a very ordinary life. _____ I get up, I take a shower and get dressed. _____ the coffee is ready, I sit down and have breakfast. Then I usually go to work. _____ I leave the house, I get in my car and drive about half an hour. However, today I'm not going to work. _____ I'm going downstairs to the pool. It's my birthday today—I'm twenty-eight years old—and I'm going to relax. Tonight some of my friends are having a party for me, so _____ I finish breakfast, I plan to go shopping for something new to wear. _____ the stores close,

2 ▶ **Answer the questions with your own information.**

1. What do you do as soon as you get up in the morning?
2. What do you do after you finish breakfast?
3. What do you usually do when you finish work or school?
4. What do you usually do in the evening before you go to bed?

3 ▶ **Complete Tom's part of the conversation.**

Alice You're in a good mood today.
Tom _____
Alice Oh, happy birthday! How old are you?
Tom _____
Alice And what are you going to do to celebrate your birthday?
Tom _____
Alice Well, have a good time.

4 ▶ **Choose *a* or *b* to complete the conversation.**

Alice You look upset. Is anything wrong?
Tom a. Yes. I found my keys. They were in my apartment.
 b. Yes. I can't find my keys. I think I locked them in my apartment.
Alice Uh-oh. You've got a real problem because the building manager isn't here.
Tom a. When will he be back?
 b. When did he leave?
Alice I don't know exactly. He went away for a week.
Tom a. What am I going to do? I can't go to a party dressed like this.
 b. What are you going to do later?
Alice I don't know. But you're right. You can't go to a party dressed like that!
Tom a. Well, I'd better call the police. Maybe they can help.
 b. Well, I'd better get ready for the party. Maybe I'll go like this.

5 ▶ **Play these roles.**

Student A B locked his keys inside his apartment. Ask B what he is going to do about his keys. If you think his suggestion is good, tell him it's a good idea. If you don't think so, suggest something else he could do. Here are some possibilities:
(1) call a friend for help,
(2) climb in a window,
(3) borrow some clothes,
(4) not go to the party.

Student B You locked your keys inside your apartment. Tell A what you will do.
Here are some possibilities:
(1) call a friend for help,
(2) climb in a window,
    (3) borrow some clothes for the party,
    (4) not go to the party.

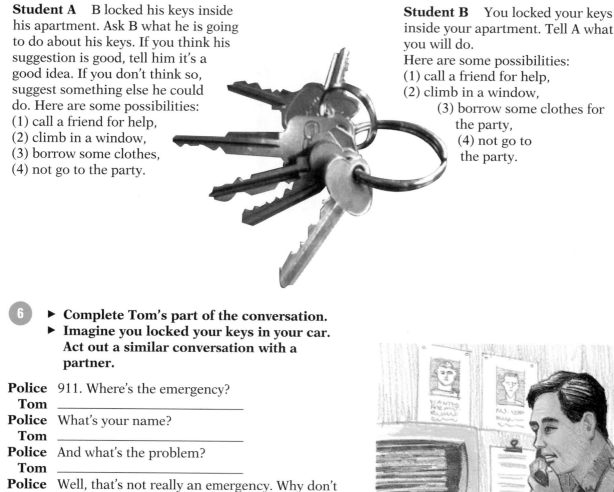

6 ▶ **Complete Tom's part of the conversation.**
▶ **Imagine you locked your keys in your car. Act out a similar conversation with a partner.**

Police 911. Where's the emergency?
Tom _____
Police What's your name?
Tom _____
Police And what's the problem?
Tom _____
Police Well, that's not really an emergency. Why don't you call a locksmith? He can open your door.
Tom _____
Police You're welcome.

7 ▶ **Tom found a list of locksmiths in the telephone directory. Listen to the phone call and choose *a* or *b*.**

1. The name of the locksmith is
   a. A. B. Goode.
   b. AAA Locks.

2. The locksmith will be at Tom's apartment
   a. after lunch.
   b. before lunch.

3. To unlock the apartment, it will cost
   a. $5.95 plus tax.
   b. $15.95 plus tax.

4. The phone call put Tom in a good mood because
   a. he can change his clothes for his birthday party.
   b. he can have a party in his apartment.

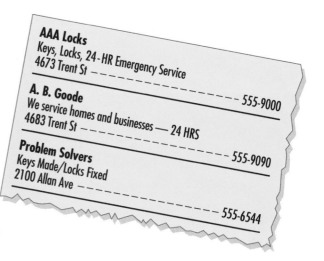

AAA Locks
Keys, Locks, 24-HR Emergency Service
4673 Trent St – – – – – – – – – – – 555-9000

A. B. Goode
We service homes and businesses — 24 HRS
4683 Trent St – – – – – – – – – – – 555-9090

Problem Solvers
Keys Made/Locks Fixed
2100 Allan Ave – – – – – – – – – – – 555-6544

8 ► **Tom's neighbors are talking. Complete each conversation, using a direct and an indirect object.**

A We need to send that birthday card to Tom right away. His birthday is today.
B Don't worry. _____ the day before yesterday.

A Hi. Could you give this package to Tom Chomsky in Apartment 44?
B Of course. _____ as soon as he comes home from work.

A Did we get any mail?
B No, only a letter for Tom Chomsky. The mail carrier _____ by mistake.

9A ► **Student A follows the instructions below.**
► **Student B follows the instructions on page 126.**

Student A You are going to Tom's birthday party, which is in an apartment building called Mason Towers. Ask your partner how far Mason Towers is and ask how you get there. Find Mason Towers on the map and thank your partner. Then give your partner directions to the place he or she asks about.

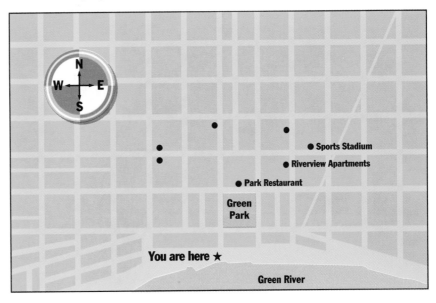

10 ► **You are at Tom's party and are talking to someone you don't know. Complete the conversation with your own information.**

A _____
B I'm from Chicago originally.
A _____
B For only three months. Are you from here originally?
A _____
B Do you have any special interests?
A _____
B Me? Well, I like to read and go to the movies.

9B ▶ **Student B follows the instructions below.**
Student A follows the instructions on page 125.

Student B Look at the map and give your partner directions to the place he or she asks about. Then ask your partner how far the Sports Stadium is and ask how you get there. Find the Sports Stadium on the map and thank your partner.

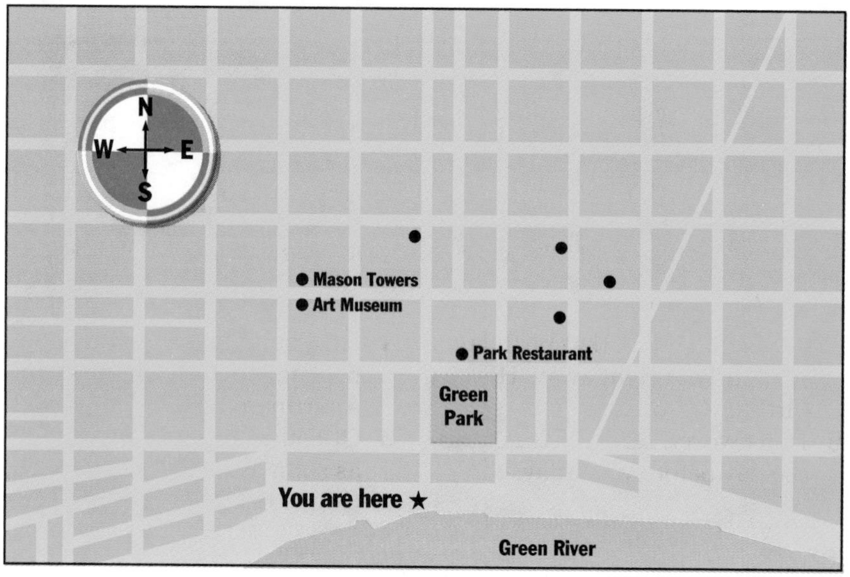

(Map showing N/S/E/W compass, with labels: Mason Towers, Art Museum, Park Restaurant, Green Park, You are here ★, Green River)

11 ▶ **Imagine you have met someone interesting at Tom's party and want to see the person again. Put the conversation in order.**
▶ **Act out a similar conversation with a partner.**

___ Fine.
___ No, I don't feel like seeing that. I don't like violent movies.
___ Maybe we could go to a movie or something this weekend.
___ Would you like to see *Lethal Weapon*?
___ Well, how about *Enchanted April*? The scenery's beautiful and it's very romantic.
___ That's a good idea. I love movies.

12 ▶ **Complete the movie review with *someone* (*somebody*), *somewhere*, *something*, *anyone* (*anybody*), *anywhere*, *anything*, *no one* (*nobody*), *nowhere*, or *nothing*.**

When you think about the title *Magic Adventure*, you think about fun, romance, good scenery, and perhaps even great music. But this movie didn't go _____ exciting—the story was boring. In fact, I don't think there is _____ positive I can say about *Magic Adventure*—there was _____ I liked about it.

The acting was terrible— _____ seemed comfortable in the role he or she played—and the music wasn't special. I guess many other people agree with me because the movie theater was empty— _____ was there! So, if you want to see _____ good—or _____ in a good role—choose another movie.

13 ▶ **Imagine you are buying two tickets for a movie and the cashier only gives you change for a ten-dollar bill. Act out the conversation with a partner.**

A Two, please.
B _____
A Excuse me. I think I gave you a twenty.
B _____

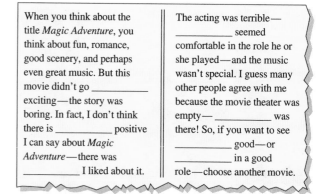

14 ▶ **Talk with your classmates.**

Tell your group the name of a movie you saw recently. Answer your classmates' questions.

PREVIEW

FUNCTIONS/THEMES	LANGUAGE	FORMS
Suggest an alternative	Let's go to a baseball game. Why don't we go to a soccer game instead?	
Make a comparison	I like soccer better than baseball. The Grand Hotel isn't as expensive as the Ritz.	Comparisons with . . .*er than, more/less . . . than,* and *as . . . as*
Make a suggestion	Should we take some food with us? Yes. It's more expensive at the stadium.	*Should*
Talk about the weather State an expectation	What's the weather going to be like on Saturday? It's supposed to get colder. It's going to be cloudy too.	*Be supposed to*
Describe someone's appearance	What does your father look like? He's a little taller than I am. He's got curly brown hair, and he wears glasses.	*Look like*
Describe someone's personality	And what's he like? He's sort of quiet, but he's very nice.	*Be like*

Preview the conversations.

These people have been to a baseball game. What spectator sports are popular in your country? Do you ever go to these games?

The man on the left is tall. He has brown hair and wears glasses. Describe the man on the right.

66. I've got an idea.

It's Saturday afternoon, and Patrick and Kate Shultz are making plans for the evening.

A

Patrick I've got an idea. Let's go to a baseball game tonight.

Kate Why don't we go to a soccer game instead? I like soccer better than baseball.

Patrick Well, for one thing, it's not soccer season.

Kate Oh.

Patrick But the Angels are playing the Bulldogs tonight.

Kate Well, O.K. Uh . . . should we take some food with us?

Patrick Yes. It's more expensive at the stadium. By the way, what's the weather going to be like tonight?

Kate It's supposed to get cooler.

Patrick I hope so. It's really hot now. . . . Oh, there's the phone. I'll get it.

B

Patrick Kate, it's my cousin Ron. He's in town on business. Is it O.K. if I invite him to the game?

Kate Of course it's O.K.

Patrick Ron? Kate and I are going to the Angels game tonight. Would you like to come with us?

Ron Yeah. That'll be fun.

C

Patrick Do you remember Ron? He was at Bill's wedding. He's Aunt Sally's son.

Kate I don't think I met him. What does he look like?

Patrick Well, he's a little taller than I am, and he's got curly brown hair. And he wears glasses. I guess he's about thirty.

Kate No, I didn't meet him. What's he like?

Patrick He's a nice guy. He's sort of quiet, but he's got a good sense of humor.

Kate Where's he staying?

Patrick At the Ritz.

Kate Really? I'm surprised. The Grand is just as convenient as the Ritz, and it isn't as expensive.

Kate Well, Ron, what did you think of the game?
Ron It was O.K.
Kate What did you think, Patrick?
Patrick I'm glad the Angels won, but it wasn't as exciting as the last game.

Figure it out

1. Listen to the conversations. Then say *True* or *False*.

1. Kate has met Patrick's cousin Ron before.
2. Kate, Patrick, and Ron went to a baseball game together.

2. Listen again and choose *a* or *b*.

1. Kate likes
   a. baseball better than soccer.
   b. soccer better than baseball.

2. The food is
   a. more expensive at the stadium than at home.
   b. cheaper at the stadium than at home.

3. Ron is
   a. taller than Patrick.
   b. shorter than Patrick.

4. Patrick thinks
   a. the last game was more exciting.
   b. the last game was less exciting.

3. Match.

1. Should we take some food with us?
2. What's the weather going to be like?
3. There's the phone.
4. Is it O.K. if I invite him to the game?
5. Would you like to come with us?
6. What does he look like?
7. What's he like?
8. What did you think of the game?

a. Of course it's O.K.
b. He's sort of quiet.
c. I'll get it.
d. Yeah. That'll be fun.
e. It wasn't as exciting as the last game.
f. He's tall and wears glasses.
g. Yes. It's more expensive at the stadium.
h. It's supposed to get cooler.

67. Let's go to a baseball game.

1 ► Listen to the conversation. Then circle *W* for the sports the woman prefers to see. Circle *M* for the sports the man prefers.

W M
1. A baseball game

W M
2. A soccer game

W M
3. A basketball game

W M
4. A tennis match

W M
5. A football game

2 ► Listen to the conversations.
► Act out a similar conversation with a partner. Use the suggestions and comparisons in the box or your own ideas.

A I've got an idea. Let's go to a baseball game.

B Why don't we go to a soccer game instead? I like soccer better than baseball.

A Well, O.K. Should we take some food with us?

B Yes. It's more expensive at the stadium.

B Yeah. That'll be fun. Should we take some food with us?

A Yes. It's more expensive at the stadium.

Some suggestions and comparisons

Should we take . . .	Yes. It's . . .
the train?	faster than the bus.
some food?	more expensive at the stadium.
something to drink?	less expensive than at the stadium.
a jacket?	not as warm as yesterday.

3 ► Study the frames: Comparisons with *. . .er than, more . . . than,* and *less . . . than*

The train is	**faster** **earlier**	**than**	the bus.	When an adjective or adverb is one syllable or ends in *y,* add *er.*

Soccer is	**more** **less** **exciting**	**than**	baseball.	When an adjective or adverb has more than one syllable, use *more* or *less* + adjective or adverb.

Notice these spelling changes.	
The bus arrived **later** **earlier** than the train.	lat¢ + *er* *y* →*ier*
The crowd was **bigger** than I expected.	When an adjective or adverb ends in a single vowel + a consonant, double the consonant before adding *er.*
Today's game was **better** **worse** than the one last week.	*Good* →*better* and *bad* →*worse* are irregular.

4 ► **Complete the newspaper article with comparisons, using the words in parentheses.**

Angels Win 7 to 4

With both teams playing very badly, last night's baseball game was certainly _____ (exciting) the last game. Angels pitcher Al Garcia's pitches were _____ (slow) usual, and the other players missed more balls than they caught. The weather didn't help either. It was much _____ (cold) it usually is at this time of year. The crowd was _____ (uncomfortable) the players—the players were busy running and hitting and catching balls—and many people left _____ (early) normal because they didn't have jackets or sweaters. Two good things about baseball games this season: Tickets are _____ (cheap) last year, and the hot dogs and hamburgers seem _____ (good). And two bad things: Parking is _____ (bad) last year—there just aren't enough spaces for everyone—and the refreshments at the food stands are _____ (expensive).

Angels pitcher Al Garcia

5 ► **Study the frame: Comparisons with *as ... as***

| The Grand | is just isn't | **as** | **convenient expensive** | **as** | the Ritz. |

Just in *just as ... as* adds emphasis to the comparison and means "exactly."

6 ► **Look at the travel brochure and compare the two hotels, using *just as ... as* and *not as ... as*. Then compare the bus and the train.**

The Grand is just as convenient as the Ritz.

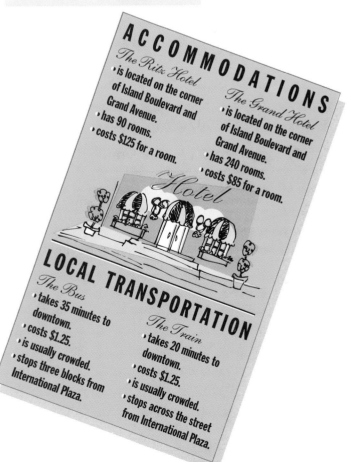

ACCOMMODATIONS

The Ritz Hotel
• is located on the corner of Island Boulevard and Grand Avenue.
• has 90 rooms.
• costs $125 for a room.

The Grand Hotel
• is located on the corner of Island Boulevard and Grand Avenue.
• has 240 rooms.
• costs $85 for a room.

LOCAL TRANSPORTATION

The Bus
• takes 35 minutes to downtown.
• costs $1.25.
• is usually crowded.
• stops three blocks from International Plaza.

The Train
• takes 20 minutes to downtown.
• costs $1.25.
• is usually crowded.
• stops across the street from International Plaza.

7 ► **Imagine you and a partner are planning a business trip. Decide where to stay and how to get to your appointments at International Plaza. Then tell the class which hotel and which form of transportation you think is better. Say why you think so.**

68. It's supposed to get colder.

1 ▸ **Listen to the weekend weather report and choose *a* or *b*.**
▸ **Look at the weekend weather map in exercise 2 to check your work.**

1. On Saturday, it's supposed to be _____ in Los Angeles.
   a. warm and sunny
   b. sunny but cool

2. The temperature is supposed to be 72 degrees. That's about _____ degrees Celsius.
   a. 72
   b. 22

3. The weather in New York on Saturday is supposed to be _____ .
   a. sunny but cold
   b. rainy and cold

2 ▸ **Listen to the conversation.**
▸ **Imagine you are in Los Angeles. Practice the conversation with a partner.**
▸ **Imagine you are in one of the other cities on the map and act out a similar conversation.**

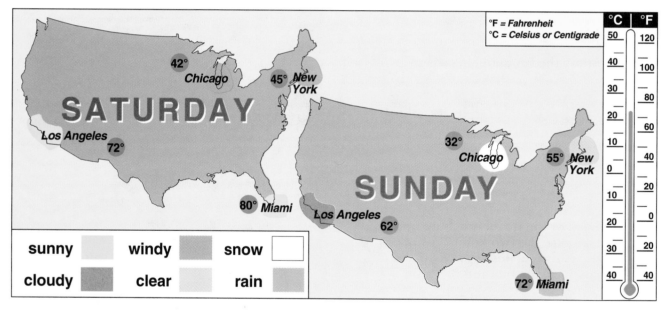

A What's the weather going to be like on Saturday?
B It's supposed to be warm and sunny.
A What about Sunday?
B It's supposed to get colder. It's going to be cloudy too.

It's supposed to . . .

get be	cooler. colder. warmer. hotter. cloudy.
rain. snow. clear up.	

3 ▸ **Talk to a classmate.**

Invite a classmate to do something after school, tonight, or this weekend. Answer your classmate's question about the weather.

A *Let's go to a soccer game tonight.*
B *That sounds like fun. What's the weather going to be like tonight?*
A *It's supposed to be nice.*

69. What does he look like?

1 ▶ **Match the descriptions with the pictures.**

1. ☐

2. ☐

3. ☐

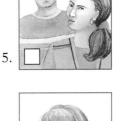
4. ☐

5. ☐

6. ☐

7. ☐

8. ☐

9. ☐

10. ☐

a. He's got curly brown hair.
b. She has short blond hair.
c. She's got long straight red hair.

d. He's bald.
e. He has a mustache.
f. He's got a beard.
g. She wears glasses.

h. He's taller than I am.
i. He's shorter than me.
j. She's about my height.

2 ▶ **Listen to the conversation.**
▶ **Practice the conversation with a partner.**
▶ **Act out similar conversations. Ask your partner about a family member, a teacher, a boss, or someone else.**

A What does your father look like?
B He's a little taller than I am. He's got curly brown hair, and he wears glasses.
A And what's he like?
B He's sort of quiet, but he's very nice.

Some ways to describe personality		
She's He's	very really	friendly. outgoing. nice. easygoing.
	sort of a little	quiet. shy. moody.

3 ▶ **Henry, George, and Bill McDonald are brothers. Work with a partner and match each person with the correct description.**
▶ **Imagine you know Henry but not George or Bill. Ask questions about one of the other two brothers.**

___ 1.

a. Henry McDonald has blue eyes and curly black hair. He's about forty, and he wears glasses. He's very outgoing and has a great sense of humor too. He's a really nice guy.

___ 2.

b. George McDonald is a little younger than Henry, and he doesn't look like him at all. He's got curly light brown hair and a mustache. He's good-looking, but he probably should lose a little weight. He's less outgoing than Henry. In fact, he's a little shy.

___ 3.

c. Bill McDonald is a little older than Henry. He has curly black hair, and he's starting to go bald. He has a beard. He's a little moody and not as easygoing as Henry.

70. Would you like to see some pictures?

Emma, Tom, Steve, and Eva are at a rock concert. During the intermission, Eva shows everyone some pictures she took with her new camera.

1

Eva Wow! That was fantastic!

Steve Yeah. They were really incredible. I hope the second half is as good.

Emma Well, it was too loud for me. How about you, Tom?

Tom To tell you the truth, I don't really care for rock music.

Eva Well, we're all glad you came with us. Hey, would you like to see some pictures? I took them with my new camera.

Tom Sure.

Eva This is a picture of Steve's soccer team.

Steve The guy holding the ball is Charley, a good friend of mine.

Tom He's pretty tall.

Emma Actually, I think Charley and Steve are about the same height.

Steve No, Charley's a lot taller than I am.

Eva Anyway, here's a picture of my chemistry teacher, Miss Edwards.

Steve She looks very nice. What's she like?

Eva She's very smart, and she has a great personality. She's probably the best teacher in the school.

Steve Oh, look! Here comes the band. . . .

2. Figure it out

Say *True, False,* or *It doesn't say*.

1. Steve and Eva are really enjoying the concert.
2. Tom thought the band was too loud.
3. Eva has a new camera.
4. Eva took a picture of Steve's soccer team.
5. Steve and Tom are about the same height.
6. Eva doesn't like her chemistry teacher.

3. Listen in

The young men above are listening to the weather forecast on the radio. Read the statements below. Then listen to the weather forecast and choose *a* or *b*.

1. The temperature in Los Angeles today is
   a. eighty degrees.
   b. seventy-four degrees.

2. Tonight, it's supposed to get
   a. a little cooler.
   b. a lot warmer.

▭ 4. How to say it

Practice the conversation.

A Tennis is more exciting than baseball.

B Yes, but soccer is more exciting than tennis.

A Oh, I think tennis is as exciting as soccer.

B Well, I like soccer better than tennis.

5. Your turn

After the rock concert, Steve invites Eva to come to his apartment and watch television. Act out the conversation. Use the information below.

Steve invites Eva to come to his apartment and watch television.	Eva accepts Steve's invitation to go to his apartment and watch television.
He wants to watch a baseball game on television.	She wants to watch a tennis match on television.
He'd like to make a chicken dinner with rice and vegetables to have while he and Eva watch the game.	She wants to eat dinner while they watch the game, too. But she'd like to go to a fast-food restaurant and get some fried chicken and french fries to go.
He'd also like to invite Charley to come over and watch television with them.	She feels tired. She would like to have a quiet evening with her brother and go home early.

ROCK

71.

It's everywhere. It's on the radio, our stereos, and Walkmans. Turn on the TV and you will probably find a station that plays rock music videos. Rock first became popular in the 1950s in the United States. Called "rock 'n' roll," it developed from a variety of different styles of music—for example, jazz, blues, and church gospel singing. Here are only a few of the many performers and groups that have made rock popular around the world.

1950s

With his first hit "Tutti Frutti," **Little Richard** demonstrated a wild and exciting style of performing that influenced many later rock performers.

Chuck Berry was the first of the great rock songwriters and his first hit record was "Maybellene." Many performers, including Elvis Presley and the Beatles, said Berry influenced their own music.

"Rock Around the Clock" by **Bill Haley and the Comets** was the first international rock hit and is still one of the best-selling records of all time.

Elvis Presley had a huge success with "Heartbreak Hotel" in 1956. Elvis went on to become one of the biggest superstars in the history of popular music.

1960s

In the 1960s, the **Beatles** were the first of many groups from England to become famous around the world. One of their first major hits was "I Want to Hold Your Hand."

Another British group that is still popular today is the **Rolling Stones**. The "Stones" showed the influence of blues in their music, and one of their hit songs was "I Can't Get No Satisfaction."

Bob Dylan sang songs about problems in the world like war and poverty. Because of his roots in folk music, his style became known as folk rock. A popular Dylan song is "Blowin' in the Wind."

Music by black singers like **Diana Ross and the Supremes** came from Detroit, Michigan, and became known as soul music. "Stop in the Name of Love" was one of their hits.

1970s

Led Zeppelin ("Stairway to Heaven") was one of the popular "heavy metal" groups of the day. Heavy metal was influenced by 60s musicians like Jimi Hendrix who experimented with the electric guitar.

Although some critics feel that rock in the 70s lost the spirit and excitement of the music of the 50s and 60s, **Bruce Springsteen** demonstrated some of the youthful energy of the previous two decades with such songs as "Born to Run " and "Thunder Road."

Reggae—the music made famous by **Bob Marley** from the Caribbean nation Jamaica— brought a new sound to rock. A popular example was the song "Stir It Up."

Donna Summer ("Last Dance") became known as the Queen of Disco. Disco music was often influenced by rhythms from Latin America.

1980s

Run D.M.C. was one of the first successful rap groups. Rap performers "talk" rather than sing the words of songs about the worries and problems of young people in a tough world.

Rock videos opened the eyes as well as the ears to music and dance. **Madonna**, one of rock's superstars, became famous for her recordings, videos, and live performances.

Michael Jackson is another name that is known all over the world. His album *Thriller* became the biggest-selling record album of all time.

Peter Gabriel and **Tracy Chapman** were among the many artists who gave concerts to promote social change in the United States and around the world.

Read the article and answer the questions.

1. Without looking at the article, name one important singer or group from the 1950s, the 1960s, the 1970s, and the 1980s.

2. Can you name any other major singers or groups that should be included in each decade?

3. What singers or groups are popular in this decade?

PREVIEW

FUNCTIONS/THEMES	LANGUAGE	FORMS
Request permission formally	May I use your phone? Certainly.	*May*
Report a lost item	I lost my passport.	
Ask for and show identification	Do you have any identification? Yes. Here's a credit card.	
Thank someone	Thank you very much. Don't mention it.	
Give advice	Just be more careful next time.	
Describe a car accident Provide information	What happened exactly? A car went through the red light. I slammed on the brakes and went off the road. Can you describe the other car? I think it was a Ford Escort. What color was it? Dark blue. Did you get the license plate number? No, I didn't.	
Express sympathy Wish someone well Say what you think	I'm sorry (that) you wrecked your car. I hope (that) your car is O.K. I think (that) you're very lucky.	*That* + noun clause
Talk about an accident	Who has had an accident? I have. What happened? I was on my bike and a car hit me.	Review: subject questions and short answers

Preview the conversations.

Have you ever had a car accident? What happened?
Did the police come to the scene of the accident?

72. Accident

 Eric and Michelle are driving home from a weekend in the country.

 A

Police officer Who's the driver of the car?
Eric I am.
Police officer May I see your driver's license, please?
Eric Yes. Here you are.
Police officer What happened exactly?
Eric Well, a car went through the red light. I slammed on the brakes, and my car went off the road and hit the sign.
Police officer Did the other driver stop?
Eric No, he didn't. He didn't even slow down.
Police officer All right. Could you come back to my car? I have to fill out a report.

B

Police officer Miss, could I have your name, please? I'm listing you as a witness.
Michelle Michelle Kelley. K-E-L-L-E-Y.
Police officer Do you have any identification?
Michelle Yes. Here's my driver's license.

C

Police officer Can you describe the other car?

Eric I don't really remember what it looked like.

Michelle Hmm . . . it was a small car. I think it was a Ford Escort.

Police officer What color was it?

Michelle Dark blue.

Police officer Did you get the license plate number?

Michelle No, I didn't.

Eric Neither did I. We're just glad that we didn't get hurt—or wreck our car.

Police officer Yeah. Well, it's a good thing you had your seat belts on.

D

Police officer All right. I think I have all the information I need.

Eric May we go now?

Police officer Sure. . . . I hope your car is O.K.

Eric Thanks. I think there's just a dent in the front.

Police officer Well, just be more careful next time.

Eric Don't worry. We will.

Figure it out

1. Listen to the conversations and choose the correct answer.

a. The accident was Eric's fault.
b. The accident was the other driver's fault.

2. Listen again. Then say *True, False,* or *It doesn't say.*

1. Eric is the driver of the car.
2. He has a driver's license.
3. The driver of the other car also has a driver's license.
4. The other car stopped at the red light.
5. The other driver was a woman.
6. Michelle saw the other driver.
7. Eric's car has a dent in the front.

3. Find another way to say it.

1. Who's driving the car?
2. Give me your driver's license, please.
3. How did it happen?
4. Come back to my car, please.
5. Tell me your name, please.
6. What did the other car look like?
7. Can we go now?

73. May I use your phone?

1 ▸ Complete the exchanges with the requests in the box.
   ▸ Listen to check your work.
   ▸ Practice the exchanges with a partner.

May I borrow your pen?	May I go to the restroom?
May I use your phone?	May I have your name?
May I join you?	May I look at your newspaper?

2 ▸ Study the frame: *May*

			Yes,	you he	**may**.
May	I he she we they	**use** your phone?	No,	you he she you they	**may not**.

In most situations, it is more common to give a reason than to say "may not."

May I use your phone?
No. I'm sorry. I need to use it right now.

3 ▸ Talk to a classmate.

Imagine you need a pen, a piece of paper, or some other item. Request permission from a classmate to borrow or use the item.

74. Do you have any identification?

1 ► Listen to the conversation. Then circle the numbers of the items the woman lost.

2
► Listen to the two possible conversations.
► Act out the conversations with a partner, using your own name.

A May I help you?
B Yes. I lost my passport.
A What's your name?
B Dorothy Foster.

A Just one second. . . . Yes. We have it. Do you have any identification?

B Yes. Here's a credit card.

A O.K. Here you are. Just sign here, please.

B Thank you very much.

A Don't mention it. Just be more careful next time.

B Don't worry. I will.

A Just one second. . . . No. I'm sorry, we don't have it. Why don't you check again in a few days?

B O.K., I will. Thank you.

3 ► Play these roles.

Student A Imagine you are a police officer at a police station. A tourist has come in to report something he or she lost. Offer assistance, find out the tourist's name, and return the lost item to the tourist. Be sure to ask for identification and to have the tourist sign for the item.

Student B Imagine you are a tourist in another city. You are at the police station because you have lost something. Tell the police officer what you lost and answer the officer's questions. Be prepared to show some identification—a driver's license, a passport, or some credit cards.

75. What happened?

1 ▶ Listen and match each conversation with the picture it describes.

2 ▶ Listen to the two possible conversations with the police officer.
▶ Act out a similar conversation with a partner.

Officer Who's the driver of this car?
Man I am.
Officer What happened exactly?
Man A car went through a red light. I slammed on the brakes and went off the road.
Officer Can you describe the other car?

Man Yes. It was a small car. I think it was a Ford Escort.

Officer What color was it?

Man Dark blue.

Officer Did you get the license plate number?

Man Yes. It was XYZ 93M.

Man No. I don't really remember what it looked like.

Officer Did you get the license plate number?

Man No, I didn't.

Some things that happen when you are driving		
A car	went through the red light. went off the road. ran into the tree. backed into me.	
There was a dog in the middle of the road.		
	I slammed on the brakes and	skidded into the motorcycle. hit the car in front of me. ran into the tree. went off the road. tried to miss the dog.

3 ► **Listen to the conversation.**
  ► **Imagine your partner told you that he or she had one of the accidents described in exercise 1. Act out a similar conversation. Make an appropriate comment to end the conversation.**

A I just had an accident.
B What happened?
A I ran into a tree and wrecked my car.
B I'm sorry you wrecked your car, but I'm glad you didn't get hurt.
A Yeah. It's a good thing I had my seat belt on.
B Well, I think you're very lucky.

Some comments

Express sympathy	I'm sorry It's too bad		you wrecked your car. you got hurt.
Wish someone well	I hope I'm glad	(that)	your car is O.K. it wasn't serious.
Say what you think	I think I guess I imagine		you're very lucky. you'll be more careful next time. you were pretty scared.

That is optional and is often omitted, especially in speech.

TALK ABOUT AN ACCIDENT • REVIEW: SUBJECT QUESTIONS AND SHORT ANSWERS

4 ► **Study the frame: Review of subject questions and short answers**

Subject questions are always asked with a singular verb.

Who knows what happened?	I do.
Who's the driver of this car?	I am.
Who's responsible for the accident?	They are.
Who can tell me about the accident?	He can.
Who else was in the car?	She was.
Who saw the accident?	I did.
Who has had a car accident?	Eric (has).
What hit you?	A truck (did).

When the answer is a noun, auxiliaries such as *is, was, do, did,* and *has* are optional.

5 ► **Work in a group and ask your classmates about accidents they have had. You can use the questions in exercise 4 or your own questions. Make comments like the ones in exercise 3 when appropriate.**

A *Who has had an accident?*
B *I have.*
C *What happened?*
B *I was on my bike and a car hit me.*
D *. . .*

76. You look familiar.

 Stacy Edwards is on her way to school when she sees steam coming from under the hood of her car. She gets off the freeway and goes to a garage near the exit.

1

Stacy Could you help me, please?

Steve Sure. What's the trouble?

Stacy I think the radiator exploded. The engine probably overheated.

Steve Let me take a look.

Stacy I hope you can fix it.

Steve (*Looks under hood*) Well, I don't think I can today. I'll probably have to order a new radiator for it.

Stacy You mean I can't use my car?

Steve No, I'm afraid not. . . . Say, you look familiar.

Stacy So do you.

Steve My name's Steve Kovacs.

Stacy Kovacs? Do you have a younger sister named Eva?

Steve Yes, I do.

Stacy She's a student of mine.

Steve Oh, then you must be Miss Edwards, her chemistry teacher.

Stacy Yes, I am. I'm glad to meet you.

Steve Glad to meet you, too. So, can I give you a ride somewhere?

Stacy Well, I don't know. Are you sure it's no trouble?

Steve No, not at all.

Stacy Well, thanks. I appreciate it. I really have to get to school.

2. Figure it out

Say *True, False,* or *It doesn't say.*

1. Stacy's car overheated.
2. Stacy drove into Steve's repair shop.
3. Steve can fix her car today.
4. Stacy has to buy a new radiator.
5. Stacy looks familiar to Steve because they have met before.
6. Stacy's going to take the bus to school tomorrow.

A woman has come to pick up her car. Read the questions below. Then listen to the conversation and answer the questions.

1. How much does the woman have to pay?
2. What kinds of identification does she have?

Practice the conversations.

1. **A** Who's the owner of this car?

   B I am.

2. **A** It's such an old car.

   B It really is.

5. Your turn

John Wilson had a car accident a few days ago, and he brings his car to Steve's shop. Steve and Bob are out to lunch, so Margaret asks him what happened. Play the roles below.

Margaret   Ask John how the accident happened. Find out about the other car and the driver. Also, ask John what the police did.

John   Describe how your car was hit on the freeway on your way to work. After the accident, you talked to the driver of the other car and found out she wasn't hurt. The police soon came and made a complete report.

A horseless carriage, 1892

Air conditioning, ABS, and air bags are common in today's cars.

In-car computers will provide information about traffic and road conditions.

There have been many changes in the automobile since the introduction of the first "horseless carriage." Among other things, we have seen the addition of power steering, power windows, air conditioning, anti-lock brake systems (ABS), and air bags to protect the driver and passenger in case of an accident. A car can even have a telephone if the buyer can afford it.

Today, automobile companies are trying to develop cars that use less gasoline—and cause less pollution. The state of California passed a law which says that by the year 2003, ten percent of the cars sold in that state should make no exhaust pollution. Consequently, there is a great deal of interest in developing a good electric car. Models of these cars—cars that make no noise and run on batteries—already exist.

Using computer technology, automobile companies and local governments are also experimenting with information systems that join together cars, highways, and central information centers: a computer in the car "reads" sensors on the road and sends information to a central area. Information about traffic and road conditions is then sent back to the in-car computer. Also, the in-car computer can help drivers figure out where they are, and how to get to their destination as easily as possible. These systems, called Intelligent Vehicle/Highway Systems (IVHS), are already being tested in cities in the United States, Japan, and certain countries in Europe.

According to *Popular Mechanics* magazine, one day highway travel will be automated from the time you get on a highway until you get off. A driver "will simply push a button on the computer inside the car and choose his destination. The computer will then find the fastest way to, say, the office, taking into account information about current traffic." The driver will still have to drive the car on local streets. However, once the driver is on a major highway or expressway, the car will drive itself.

1. Read the article. Then match the underlined words with their definitions.

1. carriage
2. pollution
3. sensor
4. destination
5. be automated
6. taking into account

a. something that is used to "read" the quantity of light, sound, noise, etc.
b. the place where you are going
c. considering
d. dirt and chemicals in the air that are not good for people
e. work without the help of people
f. a vehicle that is usually pulled by horses

2. Answer the questions.

1. What does IVHS stand for?
2. How does IVHS work?
3. Choose the best title for the article.
   a. From the Horseless Carriage to the Intelligent Car
   b. Cars that Run on Batteries and Make No Noise
   c. Today's Traffic Problems

PREVIEW

FUNCTIONS/THEMES	LANGUAGE	FORMS
Talk about plans	What are you doing this weekend? I'm not sure yet. Why? I think I'll have some people over for dinner.	Review: the future with *going to*, the present continuous as future, and the future with *will*
Invite someone	My parents are having a barbecue on Sunday. Would you like to come? O.K. That sounds nice.	
Offer to bring something	Can I bring anything? Oh, no. We already have everything we need. I could bring something to drink. Well, if you want to, but you really don't have to.	
Offer help Accept or decline help	Would you like some help with that? Oh, thanks. No, thanks. I can manage.	
Introduce yourself	You're Rick's friend, aren't you? Yes, I am. I'm Tracy, Rick's sister.	Tag questions
Continue a conversation	So, how do you know Rick? We go to school together.	
Talk about things in common	Carol works at ABC Industries. So does Tracy. Carol isn't going to school full time. Neither is Tracy.	Rejoinders with *so* and *neither*
Say good-bye to a host	You're not leaving already, are you? Yes. I have to go. But I want to thank you for everything. Well, I'm glad you could come. So am I. I enjoyed myself very much.	

Preview the conversations.

When you are invited to a barbecue, dinner, or a party at someone's home in the United States, it is very common to take something to your host or hostess—perhaps a bottle of wine, some candy, or some flowers. Is this common in your country?

78. Barbecue

 Matt Rubino and Ted Harwood work for Atlas Window Cleaners in Chicago. They're talking about their plans for the weekend.

A

Ted What are you doing this weekend, Matt?

Matt I'm not sure yet. Why?

Ted Well, my parents are having a barbecue on Sunday. Would you like to come?

Matt Are you sure it's O.K.? Your parents don't know me.

Ted Of course. They always like to meet my friends. Some of my sister's friends will be there, too. It'll be a lot of fun.

Matt O.K. That sounds nice. Can I bring anything?

Ted Oh, no. We already have everything we need.

Matt I could bring something to drink.

Ted Well, if you want to, but you really don't have to.

B

Matt Would you like some help with that?
Susan Oh, thanks. You're Ted's friend, aren't you?
Matt Yes, I am.
Susan I'm Susan, Ted's sister.
Matt It's nice to meet you. I'm Matt.
Susan So, how do you know Ted?
Matt We work together.
Susan You mean at Atlas Window Cleaners?
Matt Yeah.
Susan Do you like the work? It seems dangerous.
Matt It's O.K. It's just a temporary job.
Susan Oh? What are you planning to do?
Matt Well, I'd like to be a computer programmer.
In fact, I just registered for a computer training
course at Elmhurst College.
Susan What a coincidence! So did I. Are you
taking the intensive program?
Matt No. I work all day, so I don't have the time.
Susan Neither do I. I'm taking evening classes.
Matt Well, maybe we'll be in the same class.

C

Ted's mother You're not leaving already, are you?
Matt Yes. I have to. But I want to thank you
for everything.
Ted's mother Well, we're glad you could come.
Matt So am I. I enjoyed myself very much.
Ted's mother Good. I hope you'll come
again soon.
Matt Thank you.

Figure it out

1. Listen to the conversations. Then choose _a_ or _b_.

1. a. Susan is Ted's sister.
   b. Susan is Matt's sister.

2. a. Susan and Matt work together.
   b. Ted and Matt work together.

3. a. Susan and Ted are both going to study at Elmhurst College.
   b. Susan and Matt are both going to study at Elmhurst College.

2. Listen again and say _True, False,_ or _It doesn't say._

1. Ted's family is having a barbecue this weekend.
2. Ted's parents know Matt.
3. Susan is Ted's younger sister.
4. Matt wants to take something to drink to the barbecue.
5. Both Matt and Susan are taking a computer
   training course.
6. Matt had a good time at the barbecue.

3. Find another way to say it.

1. I don't know yet.
2. Sure.
3. Are you Ted's friend?
4. I did too.
5. I don't either.
6. I had a good time.

79. Can I bring anything?

TALK ABOUT PLANS • INVITE SOMEONE • OFFER TO BRING SOMETHING • REVIEW: THE FUTURE

1 ▶ **Listen to the conversation between Nancy and Andrew. Then answer the questions below.**
   ▶ **What are some other things people do on the weekend?**

1. What are Andrew and his girlfriend doing on Saturday? What are they going to do on Sunday?
2. What are Nancy and her boyfriend doing on Saturday? What are they going to do on Sunday?

2 ▶ **Listen to the conversation.**
   ▶ **Imagine you don't have any plans this weekend. Act out a similar conversation, accepting your partner's invitation. Use the plans in the boxes or your own ideas.**

A What are you doing this weekend?
B I'm not sure yet. Why?
A My parents are having a barbecue on Sunday. Would you like to come?
B Are you sure it's O.K.?
A Of course. It'll be a lot of fun.
B O.K. That sounds nice.

Some plans

My parents are having a barbecue.

I think I'll have some people over for dinner.

I'm planning a surprise birthday party for my sister.

My girlfriend and I are having a picnic.

My husband and I are going to the beach.

My roommate and I are having a party.

3 ▶ **Listen to the rest of the conversation in exercise 2.**
   ▶ **Have a similar conversation with a partner.**

B Can I bring anything?
A Oh, no. We already have everything we need.
B I could bring something to drink.
A Well, if you want to, but you really don't have to.

I could bring . . .	
some wine.	something to drink.
some candy.	something to eat.
some flowers.	something for dessert.

4 ▶ **Study the frames.**

Review: The future with *going to*, the present continuous as future, and the future with *will*

What **are** you	**doing** / **going to do**	after work?		We're	**going** / **going to go**	to a movie.
			Maybe	we'**ll**	**go**	

My parents **are going to have** a barbecue on Sunday. My parents **are having** a barbecue on Sunday.	The future with *going to* and with the present continuous are used to talk about plans and intentions that we have thought about before the moment of speaking.
I'**ll see** you tomorrow. I'**ll call** you soon. I hope you'**ll go** with me.	*Will* is used when we decide something at the moment of speaking.
Maybe I'**ll come** later. I'**ll** probably **come** later. I think I'**ll come** later.	*Will* is often used to talk about things that are possible but not certain.
I'**ll give** him the message for you. I'**ll have** the fried chicken.	*Will* is also used to offer help and to make requests.

5 ▶ **Complete the conversation with an appropriate form of the future and the verbs in parentheses.**

A What _____ you _____ (do) this weekend?

B Oh, no! Did I forget to tell you? I _____ (have) a picnic . . . on Saturday.

A Yes, you forgot. So, who _____ (come) to your picnic?

B Oh, I invited all of my neighbors. A few friends from school _____ (come), too.

A What about Victor and Maura?

B Oh, I forgot all about them too. And I don't have their phone number.

A I _____ (ask) them for you. I _____ (see) them tonight.

B Oh, thanks.

A Can I bring anything?

B No, I have everything.

A I _____ (bring) some soda.

B Well, if you want to. So, I _____ (see) you on Saturday.

A Yeah. I think I _____ (come) early in case you forget something else!

B Uh . . . thanks. I appreciate it.

6 ▶ **Find out what a classmate is going to do this weekend. If appropriate, invite your classmate to join you in one of your weekend activities.**

80. You're Rick's friend, aren't you?

OFFER HELP • INTRODUCE YOURSELF • TAG QUESTIONS • CONTINUE A CONVERSATION

1 ► Complete the exchanges with the offers in the box.
► Listen to check your work.
► Practice the exchanges with a partner.

Would you like some help with those chairs? | Would you like help with the kids?
Would you like help with the fire? | Would you like some help with the salad?

2 ► Listen to the conversation between Adam and Tracy.
► Imagine you are at the picnic in exercise 1. Have a similar conversation with a partner. Use your own information.

Adam Would you like some help with that?
Tracy Oh, thanks. You're Rick's friend, aren't you?
Adam Yes, I am.
Tracy I'm Tracy, Rick's sister.
Adam It's nice to meet you. I'm Adam.
Tracy So, how do you know Rick?
Adam We go to school together.

Some ways you might know someone
We go to school together.
We used to work together.
We met at a party.
I met him through a friend.

3 ► Study the frames: Tag questions

I'm late as usual, **aren't I**?	Yes, you are.
I'm not late, **am I**?	No, you aren't.
You're Rick's friend, **aren't you**?	Yes, I am.
You aren't in my class, **are you**?	No, I'm not.
He's having fun, **isn't he**?	Yes, he is.
The weather isn't very nice, **is it**?	No, it isn't.
You know my brother, **don't you**?	Yes, I do.
He doesn't know my sister, **does he**?	No, he doesn't.

We often add a tag question to a statement when we want to confirm the information in the statement: *I'm late, aren't I? Yes, you are.* However, you could also disagree and answer "No, you aren't."

Notice the irregular tag *aren't I?*

4 ▶ Complete the conversation with tag questions.
   ▶ Listen to check your work.

Carol You're one of Rick's friends, _____ ?
Tracy I'm his sister. Who are you?
Carol My name's Carol Rousseau.
Tracy You're not Claude's wife, _____ ?
Carol Yeah. How do you know Claude?
Tracy I don't really. He always calls Rick
when he needs help with his homework.
He doesn't like to study much, _____ ?

Carol No, he really doesn't.
Tracy Rousseau. That's a French name, _____ ?
Carol Uh-huh. Claude was born in Quebec.
Tracy But you don't come from Canada, _____ ?
Carol No. I'm from here.

5 ▶ Listen to the conversation. Check (√) the things Carol and Tracy have in common.

Carol and Tracy
___ work at ABC Industries.
___ don't work in a factory.
___ are going to quit their jobs.
___ registered for a computer training course.

Carol and Tracy
___ are taking classes at night.
___ aren't going to school full time.
___ will be in Computers 101.
___ love school.

6 ▶ Look at the chart in exercise 5. Make comments
about Carol and Tracy.

A *Carol works at ABC.*
B *So does Tracy.*
C *Carol doesn't work in a factory.*
D *Neither does Tracy.*

Some rejoinders		
So does Tracy.	=	Tracy does too.
Neither did Tracy.	=	Tracy didn't either.
So is Tracy.	=	Tracy is too.
Neither was Tracy.	=	Tracy wasn't either.
So will Tracy.	=	Tracy will too.
Neither can Tracy.	=	Tracy can't either.

7 ▶ Talk to a classmate.

Imagine you are meeting your classmate for the first time at a picnic or party. Find
out about your classmate. You can ask some of the questions below or questions of
your own. If appropriate, use rejoinders to provide information about yourself.

Where do you go to school?
Do you go full time or part time?
Are you in the intensive program?
What class are you in?

How do you like your classes?
Where did you study before?
Do you think you'll register for another course here?
What would you like to do when you finish?

8 ▶ Listen to the conversation.
   ▶ Imagine you are at a party and have to leave.
   Say good-bye to your host or hostess.

A You're not leaving already, are you?
B Yes. I have to go. But I want to thank you for everything.
A Well, I'm glad you could come.
B So am I. I enjoyed myself very much.

81. Congratulations!

Steve has invited Stacy Edwards to see a movie. They're supposed to meet Charley and his friend J.J. in front of the movie theater.

1

Steve	I wonder where Charley and J.J. are. The movie's going to start soon, isn't it?
Stacy	Oh, they'll probably be here in a few minutes. By the way, what does J.J. stand for?
Steve	Oh, Jennifer something. I can't remember. . . . I think you'll like her. She's studying biology at UCLA. . . . Oh, here they are.
Charley	Hi, everybody.
Steve	Hi. Stacy, I'd like you to meet Charley and J.J.
J.J.	Nice to meet you.
Charley	Yes, nice to meet you. We've heard a lot about you from Steve and Eva.
Stacy	Nothing bad, I hope.
J.J.	Oh, no. Only good things.
Charley	Sorry we're late. I had a job interview after work, and it took longer than I thought.
J.J.	He kept me waiting too.
Steve	So, tell us about the interview.
Charley	I got the job. I'm going to teach physical education at Walt Whitman High School. . . . And I'm going to coach the soccer team!
Steve	Hey, that's terrific. Congratulations!
Charley	Yeah, I can't believe it. I'm finally going to get paid for doing something I like.

2. Figure it out

Put the events in the right order.

___ Charley and J.J. met Stacy and Steve at the movie theater.

___ Charley had a job interview.

___ Charley told Stacy and Steve about the job.

___ Steve introduced Stacy to J.J. and Charley.

___ A school offered Charley a job as soccer coach and he took it.

___ Steve congratulated Charley.

___ Charley picked up J.J. to go to the movie.

3. Listen in

Steve, Stacy, Charley, and J.J. discuss the movie as they leave the theater. Each one has a different opinion of the movie. Read the opinions below. Then listen to their conversation and match each person with his or her opinion.

1. The movie was boring.
2. The movie was O.K.
3. The movie was pretty good.
4. The movie was terrific.

a. Charley
b. J.J.
c. Stacy
d. Steve

4. How to say it

Practice the conversations.

1. **A** I didn't like the movie at all.

   B Neither did I.

   A I thought it was really boring.

   B So did I.

2. **A** You're Charley's friend, aren't you?

   B Yes, I am.

   A You aren't leaving already, are you?

   B Yes, I have to.

   A Oh, come on. You don't have to leave so soon, do you?

   B Yes, I really do.

5. Your turn

Charley and J.J. are saying good-bye to Steve and Stacy. Act out the conversation.

Charley We have to leave now. J.J. has to study for a test tomorrow.

Steve _____

J.J. So are we. We had a good time.

Stacy _____

J.J. It was nice meeting you, too, Stacy.

Steve _____

Charley Good night. . . . Oh, I almost forgot. I'm having some people over for dinner tomorrow night. Would you like to come?

Stacy _____

Charley How about you, Steve?

Steve _____

J.J. Well, I hope you both can come. Bye. (*Charley and J.J. walk away.*)

Stacy So, how do you know Charley?

Steve _____

Unit 14 **155**

82.

SURVEY: Why do people go back to school?

Our survey this week asks people why they continue their education, sometimes years after they have completed high school or graduated from college. Answers unanimously suggest that the changing workplace and job security are key factors.

Henry Lopez   High School Employment Counselor

At one time, taking a class or two after school or after work depended on a person's personal motivation or interest. Today we see a change in purpose. It seems that more and more people are going back to school because they've lost a job or for job security. A lot of people hate the idea of two additional years—or more—of school, but what are they going to do? They want to get ahead—and stay ahead. I tell students when they walk out the door that they are not finished with their education.

Ann Lin   Nurse

I'm not really worried about my job. Almost everybody in the medical profession is safe these days. But I do worry about keeping up-to-date and about getting a promotion. So I take a class once in a while to keep myself informed of new medical developments and to add new skills to my résumé. It's very important. I think people in general need to continue their education to stay employed.

Jason Waldbaum   College Student

I go to a community college—you know, a two-year program—and I'm studying computer technology. I think it's important for everybody to get training, especially in computers. As for me, I'd like to be a systems analyst. But already I feel the need for an additional two years of classes at a four-year university. Then I'll have a B.A. and it will look better on my résumé. I think there is a lot of competition in the workplace, and I want to be ready.

Gloria Graham   Retiree

I've never considered going back to school. I used to work, but I'm retired now, so I don't have to worry about staying on top of things. But I guess if I had to do it again, I'd go find a place where I could get some computer training. We're coming into a technological age—well, we are already there, aren't we?—and if you don't adapt, you'll be left behind. From what I read, the most jobs seem to be available in health care and computers. I'd try to get one of those.

Grant Tilton   Unemployed Airline Mechanic

I lost my job two years ago, and I couldn't find anything else in that field. I needed to do something because I have a family to support. So I decided the only way to be qualified for a different job was to go back to school—in my case, in computer technology. That's what I tell everybody. It's not easy and it's expensive, but I don't have much choice.

Kristine Olson   Dean, California Community College

We see a lot of changes in the job market and, consequently, in people's attitudes about education. Many jobs are changing or no longer exist because companies are rethinking the way they do business. They have automated their factories and do not need many of their current employees. The key is training—or retraining, actually—to find a job in a new area. Anything in the medical profession is hot—or in computers.

1. Read the survey. Then scan the survey and find:

a. two reasons people consider going back to school.
b. two areas that are hot in the job market.

2. Discuss this question.

How do people in your country compare to the interviewees above? In other words, are they worried about losing or keeping their jobs, and do they consider it important to continue their education?

Review of units 12–14

1 ▶ Complete the weekend weather report with comparisons—. . .*er* (*than*), *more/less* . . . (*than*)—and the words in parentheses.
  ▶ Listen to check your work.
  ▶ Ask a classmate what the weather is going to be like this weekend.

Today's going to be _____ (nice) it was yesterday. It will be _____ (cloudy), so you can look forward to a clear sky. It will also be _____ (sunny) and _____ (warm). And, of course, the beaches will be _____ (crowded) yesterday now that the weather is clearing up. Fortunately, for those people who are here on vacation, the weather forecast for next week is even _____ (good) the forecast for this weekend. For a _____ (complete) report, please tune in tonight for the six o'clock news.

2 ▶ It's Saturday and the weather is going to be good today, so Nicole and her boyfriend Randy are making plans. Complete Randy's part of the conversation.
  ▶ Act out a similar conversation with a partner.

Randy _____
Nicole Why don't we go to the beach instead? I like the beach better than the park.

Randy _____
Nicole By the way, what's the weather going to be like?
Randy _____
Nicole Good. Because I don't like the beach when it's windy or cool.
Randy _____
Nicole Yes. And we should also take something to drink. Everything is more expensive at those places on the beach.

Randy _____
Nicole Say, I have an idea. Why don't I invite my new neighbor, Gina, to go with us?

Randy _____
Nicole She's a lot of fun, and she has a great sense of humor.

3 ▶ Nicole and Gina live in the same apartment building. Compare their apartments using *just as . . . as* and *not as . . . as*.

Nicole's apartment	Gina's apartment
big enough for two people	big enough for one person
kitchen—7 feet by 8 feet	kitchen—7 feet by 8 feet
living room—12 feet by 18 feet	living room—11 feet by 13 feet
bedroom—12 feet by 14 feet	bedroom—12 feet by 14 feet
very sunny	not very sunny
quiet neighbors	noisy neighbors
rent—$600 a month	rent—$450 a month

4 ▶ Nicole and Randy are driving to the beach. Listen to their conversation. Then choose the picture of Gina.

1   2

5 ▶ Nicole and Randy see an accident on the way to the beach, and they stop to help. Complete the police officer's part of the conversation.
▶ Imagine you have just seen an accident. Have a similar conversation with a partner.

Police officer _____
Nicole A car ran into that woman on the motorcycle. The car went right through a red light.
Police officer _____
Nicole It was an old car. I don't know what kind.
Police officer _____
Nicole Red.
Police officer _____
Nicole Yes. It was KLJ 88B.

6 ▶ Randy is talking to the woman with the motorcycle. Put the lines of the conversation in order.
▶ Listen to check your work.

____ Yes. I guess I can.
____ Are you all right?
____ Well, I'm sorry that you wrecked your motorcycle, but I'm glad you didn't get hurt.
____ Yes, I'm fine. But look at my motorcycle.
____ You can always fix your motorcycle.
____ Don't mention it.
____ So am I. Anyway, I'll be O.K. Thanks for your help.

7 ▶ Randy and Nicole are at the beach. Complete the conversation with tag questions.
▶ Work with a partner. Act out the conversation, answering the questions with information about a third student.

Nicole She's a student at our school, _____?
Randy _____ .
Nicole She's not from here originally though, _____?
Randy _____ .
Nicole You know her name, _____?
Randy _____ .
Nicole She doesn't go to school full time, _____?
Randy _____ .

8 ► Imagine you are at the beach with some friends. Choose one of the questions below and start a conversation with a friend. Then continue the conversation, responding to your friend's answer.

Who wants a soda?
Where do you go to school?
What are you doing tonight?
You're (name of another student), aren't you?
So, how do you know (name of another student)?

Where are you from originally?
Have you ever had an accident?
Do you speak another language—besides your native language and English?
May I borrow your sunglasses?

9 ► When Randy and Nicole get home from the beach, they find Gina sitting on the steps of the apartment building. Complete their conversation.
► Imagine you lost something. Have a similar conversation with a partner.

Gina   Oh, you're back. Thank goodness.
Nicole _____
Gina   I lost my handbag, and my wallet and apartment key were in it.
Randy _____
Gina   May I use your phone? I want to call the police.
Nicole _____
Gina   Thanks.
Randy _____
Gina   No, I don't. I lost all my identification too. But I can describe everything that's in my handbag, so I'm sure the police will give it back—if they have it.
Nicole _____
Gina   So do I. Say, did you hear about the bank robbery at the First National Bank?
Nicole _____
Gina   Here. You can read about it. I'm finished with the paper.

10A ► Student A follows the instructions below.
Student B follows the instructions on page 160.

Student A   Read the newspaper articles below.
Ask your partner questions about the robbery
to fill in the blanks.
Then answer your
partner's questions
about the fire.

Police think two students started a fire at Lincoln High School on Friday night. They drove away in a Ford station wagon, but police have only two numbers of the license plate—89. The school janitor said the two young men were both around sixteen years old. One had curly light brown hair, and the other had black hair. Anyone with further information should call 555-2948.

Police say _____ stole $10,000 from the First National Bank yesterday afternoon. He escaped in a _____ car with a California license plate, license plate number _____. According to the police description, the man is _____ around _____ old. Anyone with information should call _____.

11 ► Play these roles.

Student A   You think you'll have some people over for dinner on Saturday. Find out what B is doing this weekend and invite B to come. When B offers to bring something to drink or eat, tell B that you have everything you need.

Student B   You have no plans this weekend, so you accept A's invitation. Ask if you can bring anything. Also, find out what time you should be there.

10B
▶ **Student B follows the instructions below.**
▶ **Student A follows the instructions on page** **159** **.**

Student B Read the newspaper articles below. Answer your partner's questions about the robbery. Then ask your partner questions about the fire to fill in the blanks.

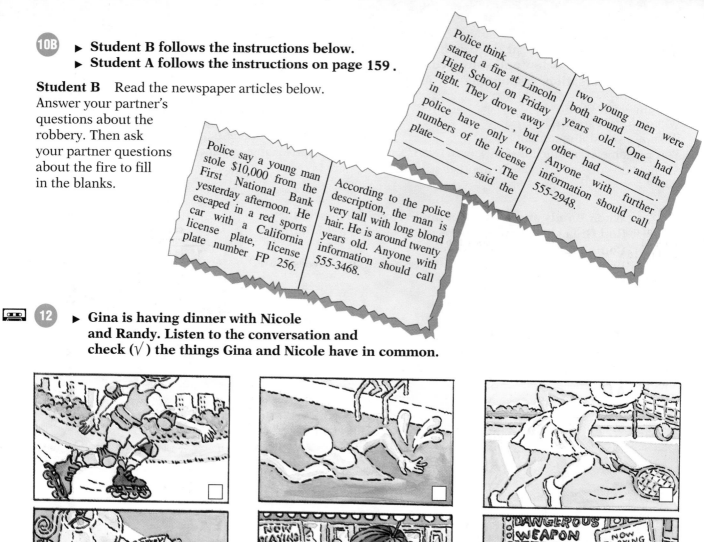

Police say a young man stole $10,000 from the First National Bank yesterday afternoon. He escaped in a red sports car with a California license plate, license plate number FP 256.

According to the police description, the man is very tall with long blond hair. He is around twenty years old. Anyone with information should call 555-3468.

Police think _____ started a fire at Lincoln High School on Friday night. They drove away in _____. The police have only two numbers of the license plate— _____ . The _____ said the two young men were both around _____ years old. One had _____, and the other had _____. Anyone with further information should call 555-2948.

12
▶ **Gina is having dinner with Nicole and Randy. Listen to the conversation and check (√) the things Gina and Nicole have in common.**

13
▶ **Find out what you and your partner have in common. Use rejoinders with *so* and *neither* when appropriate.**

A *Do you like to rollerblade?*
B *Yes, I do. Do you?*
A *I don't know how. Do you like to swim?*
B *Yes, I do.*
A *So do I.*

14
▶ **Gina is leaving and thanking Nicole for dinner. Complete Gina's part of the conversation.**
▶ **Act out a similar conversation with a partner.**

Nicole You're not leaving already, are you?
Gina _____
Nicole Well, I'm glad you could come.
Gina _____

15
▶ **Answer the questions with your own information.**

1. You're at the end of the book. Do you think you'll take another English course?
2. Which course will you probably take?
3. Are your classmates planning to take the next course?
4. What are you going to do during the break—before the next class begins?

VOCABULARY LIST

The list includes both productive and receptive words introduced in Student Book 2. Productive words are those which students use actively in interaction exercises. Receptive words are those which appear only in opening conversations, comprehension dialogues, readings, and instructions, and which students need only understand. Countries, languages, and nationalities are given in a separate list. The following abbreviations are used to identify words: V = verb, N = noun, ADJ = adjective, ADV = adverb, CONJ = conjunction, INTERJ = interjection, PR = pronoun, PREP = preposition, PAST PART. = past participle, COMP = comparative, SUPER = superlative, R = receptive. Page numbers indicate the first appearance of a word.

A

a couple of 12 R
a few 71
a great deal of 146 R
a lot 81
ability 16 R
about (PREP) 4
ABS (anti-lock brake system) 146 R
absolutely 92
Academy Award 30 R
accept 75
acceptable 103
accident 93
accommodation(s) 131 R
account (= story) 102 R
accurate 20 R
ache (N) 15
across 89
act (V) 30 R, 87
acting (N) 87
actual 14 R
ad (= advertisement) 90
adapt 156 R
add (V) 30 R
addition 146 R
additional 72 R
adjust 51
admire 76 R
admission 77 R
advertising 10 R
advertising (department) 119
advice 15 R
aerobics 45
afford 42 R
afraid 144
after all 82
again 27
age 156 R
agency 48 R
ago 97
agree (on) 61 R
agricultural 77 R
AIDS 30 R
air 53 R
air bag 146 R
air conditioner 122 R
air conditioning 146 R
airline 25
airplane 85 R
airport 37
album 136 R
alcohol 30 R
all 44
all right 94
all the way 102 R
almost 7
already 108
alternative 127 R
although 42 R
amazing 122 R
ambulance 93
among 136 R
analyst 156 R
ancient 42 R
angry 84
animal 77 R
ankle 15
announcement 19
annual 77 R

B

another 16
answering machine 50
ant 99
anti-lock 146 R
anxious 120
anybody 86
anymore 30 R
anyone 86
anything 7
anyway 134
anywhere 68 R, 81
appear 20 R
applicant 16 R
application 115
apply 119 R
appointment 14
appreciate 59 R, 151
appropriate 7 R
approximate 56 R
area 94
arm 15
arrival 22 R
as (CONJ, = when) 102 R
as . . . as 127
as a matter of fact 64 R
as soon as 85
ash 56 R
ask 104
assignment 37
assistance 141 R
assistant 4
astronaut 122 R
at all 81
at first 83 R
at least 100
at once (= at the same time) 122 R
atmosphere 56 R
attend 106 R
attention 92 R
attitude 156 R
audience 30 R
author 112 R
auto 8 R
automate 156 R
automated 146 R
automatic 122 R
automobile 85 R
available 40 R
avalanche 102 R
away (ADV) 89

B.A. 156 R
baby 78
back (ADV) 82
back (N) 96
back (V) 142
back and forth 122 R
backache 14
background 112 R
badly 131 R
baggage carousel 25
baked potato 61
balance (V) 16
bald 133
ball 6 R
band 134
bandage 20 R, 96
barbecue 147

C

barbecued 66 R
baseball 6
bath 92 R
bathtub 74 R
battery 146 R
be prepared 141 R
be supposed to 127
beard 133
beauty 30 R
because 83
bed 5
began (PAST of begin) 76 R
begin 71
beginning (N) 66 R
belief 92 R
believe 73
bench 42 R
best-selling 136 R
bet 54 R
better (COMP of good) 127
beverage 60 R
bicycle 37
bike riding 52 R
biking (go biking) 93
biking shorts 35
bill (dollar bill) 109
billion 122 R
bingo 10 R
blame (V) 56 R
blanket 102 R
blond 133
blues (music) 136 R
body 13 R
bookkeeper 9 R
bookkeeping 43
bookseller 104
bored 84
born (to be born) 30 R, 104
bottle 62
bottom 102 R
bought (PAST of buy) 90
box 72
boy (INTERJ) 54 R
boyfriend 150
brake(s) 137
branch (of a business) 4
brave 102 R
break (N) 91
break (V) 97
brief 97 R
bring 77
brochure 45 R
broiled shrimp 65 R
broken (ADJ) 94
brush (off) 102 R
budget 72 R
building 123
burn (V) 96
business 91
busy 100
but 5
butcher 66 R
button 48 R
buy 19
buyer 146 R
by the way 100

cabbage 77 R
call (N) 12 R

call (V) (= shout) 102 R
call (V) (on a phone) 89
calm 94
camera 26
camp 76 R
camping (go camping) 93
can (N) 72
can (V) 16
can't (= cannot) 16
cancer 76 R
cap 34
carbon dioxide 56 R
card 50 R, 94
care (for) (V) 134
care (take care of) 101
career 76 R
careful 137
carriage 146 R
cart 25
cartoonist 66 R
cash 109
cashier 35
cassette 25
cast (for a broken leg, etc.) 96
catch (V) 131 R
cause (V) 56 R
CD (= compact disc) 104
celebrate 123
center 25
central 146 R
ceremony 42 R
chair 38
chairperson 42 R
challenging 102 R
champion 76 R
chance 40 R
change (N) 42 R
change (N) (money) 26
change (V) 124
charge (V) 109
charity 76 R
chart 15 R
cheap 117
check (bank check) 84
check (N) (in a restaurant) 61
check (V) 27
checkbook 16
checked (ADJ) 38
checklist 119 R
chemical 146 R
chemistry 18 R, 134
chest (furniture) 38
chest (part of body) 15
childhood 76 R
chop (up) 66 R
chore 68 R
church 136 R
circle 24 R
city 44
clam chowder 65 R
cleaner (N) 149
clear (ADJ) 157
clear (up) (V) 132
clerk 75 R
client 49 R
climate 56 R
climb (V) 102 R
climber 102 R
climbing (N) 102 R

SUPPLEMENTARY VOCABULARY

IRREGULAR VERBS

Base form	Simple past	Past participle	Base form	Simple past	Past participle	Base form	Simple past	Past participle
be	was, were	been	get	got	gotten	see	saw	seen
beat	beat	beaten	give	gave	given	sell	sold	sold
become	became	become	go	went	gone	send	sent	sent
begin	began	begun	grow	grew	grown	set	set	set
bend	bent	bent	have	had	had	shake	shook	shaken
bite	bit	bitten	hear	heard	heard	shoot	shot	shot
blow	blew	blown	hide	hid	hidden	shut	shut	shut
break	broke	broken	hit	hit	hit	sing	sang	sung
bring	brought	brought	hold	held	held	sit	sat	sat
build	built	built	hurt	hurt	hurt	sleep	slept	slept
buy	bought	bought	keep	kept	kept	slide	slid	slid
catch	caught	caught	know	knew	known	speak	spoke	spoken
choose	chose	chosen	lay	laid	laid	spend	spent	spent
come	came	come	lead	led	led	stand	stood	stood
cost	cost	cost	leave	left	left	steal	stole	stolen
cut	cut	cut	lend	lent	lent	stick	stuck	stuck
deal	dealt	dealt	let	let	let	strike	struck	struck
dig	dug	dug	lie	lay	lain	sweep	swept	swept
do	did	done	lose	lost	lost	swim	swam	swum
draw	drew	drawn	make	made	made	swing	swung	swung
drink	drank	drunk	mean	meant	meant	take	took	taken
drive	drove	driven	meet	met	met	teach	taught	taught
eat	ate	eaten	pay	paid	paid	tear	tore	torn
fall	fell	fallen	put	put	put	tell	told	told
feed	fed	fed	quit	quit	quit	think	thought	thought
feel	felt	felt	read	read [rɛd]	read [rɛd]	throw	threw	thrown
fight	fought	fought	ride	rode	ridden	understand	understood	understood
find	found	found	ring	rang	rung	wear	wore	worn
fit	fit	fit	rise	rose	risen	win	won	won
fly	flew	flown	run	ran	run	write	wrote	written
forget	forgot	forgotten	say	said	said			

CLOTHING SIZES

Men

Shirts

U.S.	14	14¹/₂	15	15¹/₂	16	16¹/₂	17
Metric	36	37	38	39	41	42	43

Pants

28	30	32	34	36	38
71	76	81	86	92	97

Jackets and coats

32	33	34	36	38	40	42	44
81	84	86	92	97	102	107	112

Shoes

7	8	9	10	11	12
40	41	42	43	44	45

Women

Blouses, dresses, jackets, and coats

U.S	6	8	10	12	14	16	18
Metric	36	38	40	42	44	46	48

Shoes

5	6	7	8	9	10
35	36	37	38	39	40